COURT JUSTICE

COURT JUSTICE

THE INSIDE STORY OF
MY BATTLE AGAINST THE NCAA

ED O'BANNON
with MICHAEL McCANN
FOREWORD BY JEREMY SCHAAP

DIVERSIONBOOKS

Diversion Books
A Division of Diversion Publishing Corp.
443 Park Avenue South, Suite 1008
New York, New York 10016
www.DiversionBooks.com

For more information, email info@diversionbooks.com

First Diversion Books edition February 2018.
Hardcover ISBN: 978-1-63576-262-4
eBook ISBN: 978-1-63576-261-7

Printed in the U.S.A.
SDB/1712
1 3 5 7 9 10 8 6 4 2

CONTENTS

FOREWORD

As recently as the early 1980s, it was still possible to believe that college sports, even at their highest level, were small potatoes, at least in terms of dollars and cents, because they were. Iowa State's Johnny Orr, the highest-paid college basketball coach in the country, was making $45,000 a year, the equivalent of about $127,000 in 2017. The big football bowl games generated huge television audiences—but the rights to broadcast them went for a pittance compared to what the networks pay today. March Madness was only just beginning to take hold of the average sports fan's imagination.

Even though the pie was so much smaller, it was clear then, as now, that the athletes in the revenue-generating sports (essentially football and men's basketball) weren't getting their fair share.

As the rights fees have skyrocketed, and the coaches' salaries, and the merchandising revenue, and as the schools have built luxury boxes and weight rooms and locker rooms that would make Caligula blush, it seems more than a little precious that virtually nothing has changed for those athletes whose talents make the whole circus possible. Quarterbacks Baker Mayfield and J.T. Barrett are rewarded no more generously for their contributions to those massive money-making machines at Oklahoma and Ohio State, respectively, than Red Grange was for his efforts on behalf of the Fighting Illini in the 1920s. And everybody else—the system, the coaches, the athletic administrators, the marketing companies, the official sponsors, the shoe companies, the endowments—are flush in sweat-generated cash.

Unfair? Sure. A groundswell of outrage that might lead to change? Not really. Not, anyway, for the first 125 years of big-time college sports. The players, after all, aren't a permanent class of the disenfranchised. They cycle in and out. Any attempt on their part to tear up the system would not benefit them as individuals, only future generations. In fact, any kind of activism on their part would probably bring condemnation, or worse. And for everybody else—the schools, the NCAA, the business community, the fans—the system has been working just fine.

Then along came Ed O'Bannon. Like Curt Flood and Oscar Robertson, who paved the way for free agency in pro sports, O'Bannon decided there was a principle at stake, that he wouldn't accept the perpetual exploitation of college athletes, and former college athletes, even if the struggle would be costly. O'Bannon gave the movement to reform college sports a name and a face. More importantly, he gave it passion and purpose, animated by righteous indignation.

Maybe at some point someone else would have come along to challenge the system. Or maybe it would have taken another twenty years. Or maybe it never would have happened. It seems obvious now that someone would have made the attempt, but that wasn't inevitable. It was O'Bannon, and it still is, refusing to be cowed by those who would preserve the status quo at the expense of the athletes. This reckoning has been a long time coming—but Ed O'Bannon lit the spark that might actually lead to, believe it or not, a system that treats the athletes with the same respect it affords everyone else.

—Jeremy Schaap,
  ESPN Journalist and *New York Times* Bestselling Author
  January 2018

PROLOGUE

IT'S IN THE GAME

E

A

Sports

It's in the game.

Take it from me, "it" sure is in the game.

• • •

"Ed, you've got to believe me, Spencer was playing *you* in this video game last night."

Spencer Curtis was a nine-year-old boy in April 2009. He possessed otherworldly hand-eye coordination—back then while holding an Xbox 360 controller and in the years that followed while showing his stuff on the football field. These days he's lining up as a wide receiver for the Weber State Wildcats. When I met Spencer, I just knew him as Mike Curtis's kid. Like me, Mike was an ex–basketball player working as a car salesperson in Nevada. We had played ball against each other in the 1990s. I was a UCLA Bruin. Mike banged the boards for the University of Nevada at Las Vegas (UNLV), the college I had wanted to attend.

The video game came up in conversation within a minute of my arrival at Mike's house in Summerlin. Along with our friend Rick Glenn, Mike and I had just played in a charity golf tournament. Now it was time for a couple of beers. It was a hot, lazy Saturday afternoon in Nevada. Just like a lot of afternoons there.

But this one would prove very different.

We could all hear Spencer somewhere in the house playing his Xbox at high volume. There were beeps, slashes, and whooshes, along with ambient music. Regaining my focus, I replied to Mike, "Wait, what? Dude, you pulling my chain? How was he playing me in a video game?"

I'm not a gamer. My prime years as a video game player occurred back in the early 1980s when my brother Charles and I would spend hours on our Atari 2600 moving Pac-Man through a maze or blasting asteroids. I realized that games had evolved quite a bit since then, but why the heck would *I* be in a game? I'm no Pitfall Harry jumping over crocodiles. I'm not Frogger trying to avoid becoming roadkill. I'm just Ed.

"Yeah," Mike assured me, "Spencer has this game where you're in it. And he scored like two hundred points playing as you. You're the star, man, just like in the old days!" I was genuinely stumped. But then again, I knew next to nothing about college basketball video games. I had never played them, and my children hadn't either. I knew vaguely of sports video games like *John Madden Football* and some NBA games. They looked pretty cool, too, in their ads. But I had always assumed the players in those games gave their permission to appear and were compensated, too. Yet no one had ever asked me to be in a game.

How'd I end up "in the game"?

After my initial confusion, I started to feel like anyone would feel if they'd been Super Mario-ed: flattered. "Wow," I told Mike. Then Rick, who was sales manager where I worked, interjected with an "Ed, that's really cool, man" kind of remark.

Mike brought us over to the living room where Spencer was killing on-screen zombies. Spencer had no idea we were there. He was almost in an Xbox trance, as though his brain had been transported to the video game world. That's how realistic and immersive these games have become. "Hey, Spence, do me a favor—can you swap games and put the NCAA one in? Mr. O'Bannon wants to see himself." Spencer obliged, and we sat on the family room couch in front of the big TV with the Xbox 360 connected to it.

From the floor, Spencer grabbed the *NCAA March Madness 09* video game case—the one with Kevin Love pictured on the cover. After the disc slid into the game system, it loaded up. First the words *Electronic Arts* appeared, and then I heard, "E. A. Sports. It's in the game." After several more seconds of loading, a "select team" menu came up. Spencer—wisely—chose the UCLA Bruins 1994–95 squad.

And then, there I was, in the starting lineup. Number 31. Six feet, eight inches. Two hundred twenty-two pounds. Power forward. Left-handed shot.

The digital avatar looked a lot like me. Now, my name wasn't there—though years later we'd learn in pretrial discovery that all of the players' names were included and then removed by Electronic Arts right before they published the game. But name or not, it was obviously me.

And man, what a realistic game.

Taking a jump shot on March 5, 1995, against Louisville. EA Sports made a digital version of me from this season. (© RVR Photos-USA TODAY Sports)

It had actual Division I coaches and their names. And the courts, with light shining on the parquet, looked so real. Then there was the crowd with unique-looking fans, some with their faces painted, wearing their teams' colors and holding signs. Plus, the game nailed all of the key sounds of basketball—the rhythm of dribbling, the chaos of sneaker squeaks, the suddenness of player yells, you name it. Graphically, the players really popped out, too. They looked so lifelike, with shadow effects and facial expressions. The animation of their movement was so fluid. If you were sitting several feet away from the TV you'd honestly think that you were watching an actual broadcast of a college basketball game.

And if you closed your eyes, you would believe that an actual game was on. The crowd cheered at the right times with real crowd audio. The in-game "TV" analysis was spot on. Brad Nessler of CBS Sports provided the play-by-play while Erin Andrews of Fox Sports offered updates. The clincher? Dick Vitale—the legendary Dick Vitale—provided commentary.

"Get out of the way, baby, that was absolutely sensational!"

That's what digital Dick Vitale actually said within a few minutes of Spencer starting up the game.

This was big time. This was so real.

Spencer had "us"—my digital UCLA teammates and me—play against the 1993–94 Arkansas Razorbacks, a precursor to the team we would beat the following year for the NCAA title.

After a few minutes of watching, I was really getting into it. "Hell yeah!…That's what I'm talking about!" I made these statements to no one in particular. I was, as EA likes to say, "in the game." I saved my loudest roar for when Spencer had Tyus Edney, my point guard, pass to me for a dunk over Corliss Williamson. "Bring. It. ON!"

At that point I was thinking, *Who* doesn't *want to be in a video game?* I was going back in time to the '90s and loving every second of it. But then Mike, kind of jokingly and with absolutely no ill intent, nudged me and said, "Dude, can you believe I paid sixty bucks for this thing?"

It may have been a side-of-the-mouth comment for Mike, but it got my mind racing. "No, man," I responded. "I can't. That price is steep." Mike then gave the ol' buddy slap to my shoulder and said, "It is kind of crazy you're not getting a penny from it, but that's life. What are you going to do, you know?" He gave a laugh and was back to watching the game.

Sixty dollars. Every one of these games sells for sixty freaking dollars. God knows how many they've sold. It's crazy.

I looked away from the TV and out a window. There was something uncomfortable happening, even as I heard digital Dick Vitale continue to say complimentary things about my avatar, this "it." That "it" was *me*.

Damn.

I drove back to my home in Henderson and told my wife, Rosa, about what I had seen, but I didn't make a big deal of it. I went back to work the next morning and put it out of my mind.

A few weeks later, everything would change.

CHAPTER 1

THE CLARION CALL

I SELL CARS. AMONG OTHER THINGS, THAT MEANS I GIVE OUT MY cell phone number to a lot of people. Hopefully some of those people end up buying a car from me. It was no surprise when my phone rang that morning in early May 2009 while I was sitting at my desk at Findlay Toyota in Henderson, Nevada, looking over details about new cars coming in. But I was pleasantly surprised by the area code: 818 is Los Angeles. I'm an LA guy through and through. I know my people.

I also knew the name of the caller.

"Hello?" I answered.

"Mr. O'Bannon, how are you, my friend?"

The voice was like no other. Despite being 818, it was East Coast. It was fast. It was endearing. It was Mr. Sonny Vaccaro.

I knew Mr. Vaccaro—and he will always be Mr. Vaccaro to

me—from the summer between my sophomore and junior years in high school. I attended Nike's annual Academic Betterment and Career Development (ABCD) camp, which Mr. Vaccaro and his wife, Pam, ran at Princeton University. The camp featured high school basketball stars from across the country. They were there by invitation only. It was at Princeton where I realized I had a chance of becoming an NBA player. I was even named most valuable player of Mr. Vaccaro's camp in 1988. Back in the day, Mr. Vaccaro would tell me, "You have a chance to do something really special, Eddie. But you need to take basketball seriously. Don't blow it."

You can bet I listened to him. He was the man who brought Michael Jordan to Nike. He's the one who brought Patrick Ewing and Alonzo Mourning to Georgetown and other young stars to other big schools. He's the one who made college coaches rich by paying them to instruct their players to wear Nike sneakers. Years later, he'd work on behalf of Adidas and then Reebok with the same core mission. There's a reason why he's known as "The Sole Man." He's the real deal.

Mr. Vaccaro also "fought the fight" for young basketball players. He demanded that players receive part of the pie of wealth generated by their labor. He knew about amateurism rules that told those players "No you cannot," but he didn't care.

The methods and consequences of this kind of philosophy are dramatically different these days. Last September, Department of Justice officials announced that they were prosecuting sneaker executives, college coaches, and investment advisors for bribery, fraud, and other felony charges. The Justice Department's basic theory is that college coaches bribed or received bribes to influence where star recruits would attend college and whom college stars would hire as NBA investment advisors. We're not talking about free sneakers and discounted apparel here. Nor is this about rinky-dink NCAA violations. This concerns hundreds of thousands of dollars changing hands in alleged payoffs. And it concerns educated, middle-aged men allegedly breaking federal criminal statutes. If these guys are convicted—and none of them have been as of this writing—they could spend decades behind bars.

It was reported in the *New York Times*, the *Washington Post*, *Sports Illustrated*, and more. And some heavy hitters in college basketball have been charged. Among them are Adidas director of global marketing Jim Gatto—the point man for huge sneaker deals—and Auburn University associate head coach and former NBA rookie of the year Chuck Person. Although he wasn't charged with a crime, Rick Pitino was fired as head coach of the University of Louisville in the aftermath of the indictments. Prosecutors claim that an unnamed recruit—widely reported to be Brian Bowen, a five-star recruit—received $100,000 in inducement money to attend Louisville.

Pitino says he never knew about it.

Hmm.

Look, I realize it's too early to know where this case is headed. The defendants have hired top defense attorneys, who insist that the government is trying to unfairly criminalize NCAA rules. The charges may or may not stick, and it will be quite a while before we know how it all shakes out. Even if these guys go down in court, there will be appeals. The end game is years away. Still, I wonder if these so-called bribes were at least partly the result of amateur players not being fairly compensated. If players were able to use their own likenesses and be paid for their own brands, maybe some of these under-the-table transactions wouldn't have transpired.

Imagine that kind of world for a moment.

Instead of being stigmatized for taking under-the-table bribes, these young men—almost all of whom are black—would receive royalties and fees *over* the table. Then they would lawfully report those payments to the IRS. You know, like the rest of us do each year with our taxes? Heaven forbid the NCAA let young athletes become legitimate earners of money.

Anyway, back when I played, "bribes" and "payoffs" weren't in style, but we did see free sneakers and other people picking up the tab for meals. Ultimately, that very approach to "giving" cost Mr. Vaccaro his high-paying jobs. Sneaker companies began to view Mr. Vaccaro more as a conduit for social disruption and less as a facilitator of new business. Over time he'd also become unpopular with journalists who enjoyed close ties to the NCAA. They'd badmouth him in articles and try to connect him to corruption. My fellow young basketball players and I, however, believed in Mr. Vaccaro. We trusted him. He looked out for the interests of others when doing so was to his personal detriment. So, again, when he talked basketball, you can be darn sure we listened.

But Mr. Vaccaro was more than just a basketball guidance counselor to me. He's one of those "very important persons," if you know what I mean. I got the impression that he doesn't talk to irrelevant people and certainly doesn't suffer fools. Over the years we had lost touch. Then in 2007 we ran into each other at a high school basketball tournament he had organized in Vegas. From that point on we'd periodically call each other to say hello so we wouldn't lose touch again.

Well, that day on the phone in my office, after we exchanged pleasantries, Mr. Vaccaro revealed that he wasn't just calling to catch up. "So, Eddie, I'm actually calling with an idea that I want to run by you. Now, hear me out."

"Okay, sure, Mr. Vaccaro, I'm listening."

"You know those video games with college basketball players and those ESPN Classic broadcasts and all of those trading cards?"

"Ahh, yeah, why?"

"So I've been talking to some lawyers and I'm thinking about suing the NCAA and Electronic Arts, the company that makes those games. You see, former players—like you; I've seen you in these games—should have been getting paid for their images and likenesses all these years."

I'm not sure if Mr. Vaccaro heard me chuckle about the coincidence. "It's funny you say that," I told Mr. Vaccaro, "because a few weeks ago I saw myself in this video game and I was like, 'What the heck is this?'"

Mr. Vaccaro then asked me to share all of the details about my encounter with the Curtis family and their Xbox 360. He also revealed that he had already reached out to a number of former college basketball stars to see if they would be willing to serve as the lead plaintiff. He hadn't found any takers—yet.

"Eddie, the thing is, *you* should be the lead plaintiff. You're the perfect guy for this. You were a superstar in college, you're educated, you have a successful postplaying career, and you've always been a good guy, a family-first guy. And you know firsthand that you've been wronged. You've seen it with your own eyes."

I had seen it with my own eyes. And it's not just a video game, either. I had seen it during my time at UCLA.

• • •

Before I go further I should acknowledge something important: my four years at UCLA were awesome. I met Rosa there, and I started a family while I was there, too. I made lifelong friends that are some of the best people I've encountered. Plus, as a star athlete, there are certainly fringe benefits. You grab the attention of the beautiful girls (and at UCLA, there are a lot of them!). You get to jump in front of the line at the cafeteria and at clubs. People you don't know at all throw parties for you and make you out to be a national hero because you're good at basketball.

From the 1993-94 season, playing against North Carolina State. (© RVR Photos-USA TODAY Sports)

Everyone walking by you on campus says hi and smiles because they know who you are and they want you to be their friend.

My time at UCLA included being captain of a team that won a national title in 1995. The title run began immediately following the 1993–94 season, which had a very disappointing ending. We started that season like gangbusters, winning our first fourteen games. We really believed we'd win the national championship. ESPN and other national media thought so, too.

But we were upset by Tulsa in the first round of the 1994 March Madness tournament. Our fans were shocked. We felt embarrassed, especially by the way we played defense—or, more accurately put, didn't play defense. *Never again*, we pledged.

To that end, in the summer between my junior and senior years, I took my game to a different level. Instead of shooting a thousand shots a day, I didn't stop shooting until I *made* a thousand shots. I basically lived in the gym, with specific purpose, two goals, and two visions: to lead my team to a national championship and to be named college basketball player of the year.

I also committed to undertaking a greater leadership role. I had been the captain of my high school team and knew how to lead. We needed a leader, too. At times, our game was more like that of five individual guys who happened to be wearing the same style of uniform than that of a team of five. I also thought some of our younger guys would benefit from constructive criticism. Some of them wanted to freelance on the court for individual stats more than do whatever was necessary to help us win. I knew it all might make me unpopular. But instead, my teammates responded by naming me one of the captains going into the 1994–95 season.

I remained focused on basketball as the fall semester arrived. You may be wondering how I found time to study. I'm not going to lie—after basketball, there wasn't much in the way of study

A photo from our post-NCAA Championship visit to the White House.

time. But I attended my classes and, by and large, did my readings and did fine.

The school, of course, had an incentive to make it all work. Under NCAA rules, college athletes must take a full course load and must maintain at least a 2.0 grade point average. UCLA, like other schools, used "clustering" to help make that happen. Athletes were encouraged, if not, for all practical purposes, required, to take less-than-challenging classes that are scheduled around games and practices. Clustering has been going on for years at basically every college with a major sports program. Through this concept, college athletes find ways to balance fifty hours a week of sports work with a full-time class schedule.

I remember this way of life like it was yesterday. I spent far more than fifty hours a week on basketball, that's for sure. And in truth, I loved almost every minute of it—especially during our magical 1994–95 season. We went 31–2 that year and finished by winning 19 straight. It ended when we defeated the University of Arkansas Razorbacks in the NCAA championship game. What a way to spend my senior year of college.

• • •

Our winning streak began after we had suffered an embarrassing midseason loss at home to Cal Berkeley. On the evening
of January 28, 1995, more than twelve thousand Bruins fans
watched us stink up the joint. Two days earlier, we had pulled
out a rough, slug-'em-out win against Stanford. Maybe we were
tired. Maybe we had underestimated Berkeley. Either way, they
had a chip on their shoulder that should have woken us up.

But it didn't.

Everything we did that night was a step too slow or a jump
too short. It was like we were stuck in the mud and couldn't
figure a way out. Eventually frustration set in, and it came from
our captain: me. I directed it at one particular teammate. His
name was Charles. He was a sophomore and our starting small
forward.

He was also my brother.

It all came to a head when Charles was dunked on. He
should have been angry. He should have yelled. Heck, I would
have taken a smirk or even a frown. Instead, Charles had this
nonchalant expression on face that communicated, "I don't give a
damn." Man, it raked my nerves to no end. I needed to blow up.
Unfortunately for my brother, he would be my target.

The opportunity to explode came when our coach, Jim
Harrick, called a timeout. As we walked over to the sidelines, I
grabbed Charles's arm and got right up to his ear. With our teammates, coaches, and thousands of strangers watching, I screamed,
"Man, what the hell is your problem? You need to wake the f—
up! I raised you better than this!"

Now, I hadn't raised Charles like a parent—our parents did
that. But when Mom and Dad were at work, Charles was my
responsibility. And he understood what I meant. I had taken him

January 6, 1994, posing with my brother Charles (far left), and my parents Madeline and Ed, Sr. (© Richard Mackson-USA TODAY Sports)

to the playgrounds when we were kids. We had played with the "cats" in the neighborhood. He knew the right way to play and he sure wasn't doing that.

Charles got real upset after I got in his face. Tears welled up in his eyes and that almost never happened to him. But then he regained his composure, clenched his jaw, and looked like he was ready to tear somebody's head off.

It would be another decade before Denzel Washington starred in the movie *Man on Fire*. But on that night in 1995, and for the rest of the season, Charles was *that guy*. He was truly a man on fire. Indeed, Charles became our backbone for the next few months—our heart and our soul, if you will. He was our stopper on defense and would lock down the other team's best perimeter offensive player. He rebounded extremely well, too, and was fearless going for the boards. Charles always played above the rim, flying up and flying down. And, man, could he hit open jump shots—he had such a beautiful stroke.

So we went on a roll for the rest of the season and never looked back. That's not to say it was without bumps. During the NCAA tournament we were the number-one seed in the West Bracket. In the second round we faced an eight-seed University of Missouri team that did one thing extremely well: shoot the ball. Our game against the Tigers was one where we played well but still almost lost. We contested their shots, but they just kept draining threes or driving right by us. I remember trying to stop Paul O'Liney on one particular play. Paul was an impressive kid. He rose from being a walk-on to being the team's superstar. Late in the third quarter, I literally had both hands on his face, for like twenty-eight seconds. Then I slipped ever so slightly, and he blew right past me like Jordan. O'Liney was something else that night. If this had been a video game, he would have been on fire.

But we still pulled it out. And we can thank our lightning-quick point guard, Tyus Edney, for that. We were trailing by one point with 4.8 seconds to go on the game clock. Missouri thought they had an upset wrapped up. Then Tyus sprinted coast-to-coast and saved our season. He covered ninety-four feet in less than five seconds. To cap it off, Tyus took to the air from the paint and then, without a hint of desperation, banked the ball high off the backboard. Two points. Buzzer rings. UCLA 75. Missouri 74. We had practiced the play, and it was based on Jerry West's days with the Lakers. To see it executed so perfectly and at such a critical moment was truly special.

So we didn't lose our focus or get dispirited. That's how championship teams handle adversity. No team cruises to a title. Sometimes there are serious roadblocks. You need to stick together and that's what we did.

And we sure had a cohesive and talented team. Take Tyus. He was one of the best point guards in the country and badly underrated by the so-called experts. On defense, Tyus could put on a full court press by himself. On the other end, he was like a running back weaving through defenders, shifting left, shifting right. Nobody could stop Tyus, who grew up near me in Los Angeles. If Tyus could be a superhero, he would definitely be The Flash. Toby Bailey also stood out. He had a high basketball IQ and could guard anyone. Toby played a cerebral game that made his teammates better. Then there was our center, George Zidek. He was seven feet tall and weighed 275 pounds of pure muscle. Let's just say George took up a whole lot of space! He was really light on his feet, too, and could shoot with either hand. He had such a beautiful shot from fifteen feet out.

Coach Harrick's basic offensive scheme capitalized on all of our strengths. Typically, we'd hit the fast break with Tyus pushing it up the floor while looking to strike fast. I would usually trail down the middle of the court.

On most plays, the first option was for Tyus to see if George was open for a fifteen-foot jump shot or an easy post up under the basket. The truth is, a lot of guys didn't want to get in front of George. He was truly intimidating at his size, and he looked like a dude who could cause you serious injury if you were what stood between him and the hoop. Plus, unlike a lot of guys his size, George could drain free throws at a high rate. As a matter of fact, George would often challenge Tyus to a free throw shooting contest after practice and he'd usually beat him. That skill made him an even more potent weapon. He'd get fouled with some regularity and then go to the free throw line and get us two points.

But if our opponent stopped George, Tyus would flip it back to me as a secondary fast break option. I'd look to drive to the basket or pop back and hit a three. If I was covered, we'd shift to a half-court offense and get Charles and Toby involved. It wasn't rocket science, but it sure worked.

Our defensive philosophy was pretty simple, too. We wouldn't let you score, but if you did, it was like Ice Cube's dad, played by John Witherspoon, in the movie *Friday*: "That's yo' ass, Mr. Postman!" By that I mean, if the other team scored, we'd push it right back up their throat. It was a natural style for us. It was how three of us—Charles, Tyus, and me—played at Victoria Park in Carson City, California, as kids. It was playground style, to be sure, yet there was an ingenious method to the madness.

Our team was special in other ways, too. One of our bench players was a six-foot-seven walk-on from the Bay Area by the name of Bob Myers. Although he hardly appeared in games, Bob was a dominant practice player. He was always hustling and diving for loose balls. He was one of those guys whom you hated to play against because he would bust your butt and make you look bad if you took a play off. Coaches loved Bob because he always pushed us and made us better. Bob didn't say much, in part because he was always studying in his free time. He did okay for himself, I'd say. He's now the architect of one of most dominant franchises in NBA history: the Golden State Warriors.

Our student manager likewise did well for himself. Tony Luftman was so young he couldn't grow a beard! These days he's a lead commentator on the NHL Network. He does play-by-play in Major League Baseball, too. Back then I told him he would have his own show. I'll take credit for that one! But for most of my teammates, it was hard to predict the kind of professions they would enter, or, for that matter, the kind of husbands and fathers they would become. I'm impressed that all of them have done well. I realize that is not always the case—it's a myth to think that every college athlete can juggle being a full-time athlete with being full-time student. Some come out okay. Others don't. Back then, though, I didn't perceive a problem with this kind of arrangement between college sports and me. I realized that my education was free because I was really good at basketball. I understood the situation and why I was there. I did all I could to make studies work with my college basketball career.

The highlight of my college basketball experience occurred on April 3, 1995, at the Kingdome in Seattle: the NCAA championship game. Our opponent: the Arkansas Razorbacks, who were defending their title from the previous season.

I had been preparing my whole life for this game. It felt like it was destiny. The blood, the sweat, and the tears that I had shed—they had all gotten me to this point. There was no way in hell that we were going to lose. I just couldn't see it. In fact, when we boarded the plane to fly from LA to Seattle for the Final Four, I had this thought in my mind and feeling in my gut that I would die before we lost that tournament.

And my game was on point. It was one of those nights when the rim seemed enormous. My shot was falling from everywhere. The stadium and shooting background were comfortable, too. I ended up scoring thirty points and grabbing seventeen rebounds. More importantly, we played unselfishly, making the extra pass on offense and switching on defense. I couldn't have been prouder of those guys. And for that matter, the more than twenty-seven million people who watched the game on TV couldn't have gotten a better impression of UCLA and our basketball program. We were all Bruins that evening. Our 89-to-78 victory would be recorded in the history books and never forgotten.

The night was capped with my cutting down the net as my teammates watched from below. The image became the cover of *Sports Illustrated*, with the reading line *Return to Glory: Ed O'Bannon Celebrates UCLA's National Title.*

Talk about being on top of the world. I was standing right there.

So, no, I'm not writing this book to claim that I had a miserable college experience. It was anything but. I am writing this book, though, to reveal what motivated my lawsuit and why I hope it will spark change in college sports. And as much as I enjoyed my time at UCLA, the culture of college sports and the way the NCAA treats college athletes need fixing.

During the Bruins' championship season more than 163,000 people bought tickets to attend our home games. Many were students, families, and alumni. Some were local residents who had become UCLA fans. And though attending a Bruins game wasn't quite like going to a Lakers game, we had our fair share of celebrities in the house. Jack Nicholson, John Lithgow, Flea, and Gallagher—remember the watermelon guy?—would all occasionally show up. Plus, from TVs in homes and sports bars, millions of UCLA fans watched our games—and the commercials that aired during our games. All those people saw us advance to the tournament and saw me lead the team in scoring, rebounds, and minutes played.

And yet the system only cared that I maintained a certain grade point average in my courses so that I could spend dozens of hours each week on basketball. It cared that I stayed out of trouble and didn't stir any controversy. It cared that I cared about basketball. It cared that I helped our team win.

But it didn't care about me.

So many NCAA policies—the high-level and the petty—always struck me the wrong way. College players, a disproportionate number of whom are black, were denied certain living necessities and educational opportunities that were given to non-athletes. Meanwhile, these athletes sacrificed their bodies—and for football players, perhaps their brains, too—for the sake of the school. And it wasn't like UCLA or its athletic officials were morally opposed to helping out the athletes. They just didn't want to run afoul of the NCAA. It's about getting just a tiny, tiny slice of a massive pool of NCAA money in proper return for your valuable, dedicated work on behalf of the school so that you can live the higher-educational life of a normal college student.

So, I knew back then that if one day I had an opportunity to change the way college sports work, I'd do it. I couldn't back down. The twenty-year-old Ed O'Bannon would have been seriously disappointed in the thirty-six-year-old Ed O'Bannon had he chosen the easy path and walked away from the righteous fight.

• • •

"I like the sound of this, Mr. Vaccaro, and I'm very honored you'd think of me for it. But I need to talk to the family first."

In May 2009, when I was thirty-six years old, I had a solid job in the auto industry and a good amount of money saved from a twelve-year career in pro hoops. Rosa was, as she still is now, working as a department head in a school district, and we were raising our three children—Aaron, Jazmin, and Edward III—while living in a comfortable Las Vegas suburb.

I had it pretty good. I was Ed O'Bannon: loving husband,

father of three great kids, and a former college basketball star and NBA lottery pick. People remember me from UCLA, where I won the John R. Wooden Award in 1995 as the best player in men's college basketball. I was also "that guy" famously photographed taking down the net when UCLA became national champion in 1995. I had this identity that a lot of people would covet and do everything to protect. If I sued, if I were the lead plaintiff in a lawsuit against the NCAA, what would that mean for my family? There was a lot to process.

Mr. Vaccaro understood, and we agreed that I'd call him in the next day or two. "Take as much time as you need, Eddie. But I really think you are the perfect person for this."

When I got home from work, Rosa and I talked, and we kept talking deep into the night.

The most important consideration was our kids. Our then thirteen-year-old daughter, Jazmin, was going to be recruited to play Division I basketball. And though our youngest, Edward III, was only eleven years old at the time, he already showed a great deal of athletic promise in both basketball and baseball. Rosa and I feared colleges would blackball them if I sued the NCAA. That's how the NCAA works. We knew it well.

I also wondered about the hate mail—not the mail directed at me, I was fine with that—but what would be directed at Rosa and the kids. I wouldn't stand for that. And I knew it could get ugly, too. I would be a black man taking on the system. One need not be a historian to realize what that can lead to. If a white former player with a background similar to mine had brought the case, the optics would be a lot different. The level of social resistance, the context of the central argument that players should have say over their names, images, and likenesses—all of it would be viewed through a different lens. Look, race isn't just about color. It's also about the associations and shared experiences that come along with one's race. A black man saying he was wronged triggers all sorts of feelings. I'd be subject to them. So would my family. That concerned me.

But my past also ran through my head. That night I replayed in my mind so many conversations and events from over the years. I remember being in study hall at UCLA and talking with teammates about how people were paying all this money to watch us play and we weren't getting any of it. We knew if we complained, they would be upset. So we kept quiet and kept our heads down.

That was wrong. And now I had an opportunity to speak up for athletes. I had a chance to take on those older, out-of-touch and mostly white guys from a completely different world. They sit and judge young men whom they know nothing about—they don't know anything about us. They don't know what college athletes have lived through and what they go through on a daily basis. And yet they pass judgment like arrogant professors and impose rules on college athletes like they're "the help."

Enough.

After no sleep, I called Mr. Vaccaro early the next morning. I didn't worry about what time it was because I was (and remain to this day) convinced that this man never sleeps.

"Hello?"

"Good morning, Mr. Vaccaro."

He knew my voice. "Good morning, Eddie, I've been eagerly awaiting your call. How are you, my friend?"

"I'm well, thank you. So, Mr. Vaccaro, Rosa and I talked about this lawsuit idea all night." He quickly jumped in. "Okay." At that point, I'm pretty sure Mr. Vaccaro thought I was going to tell him no. He probably figured our family was in a comfortable place in life and we didn't need to upend everything. "We feel blessed to have this opportunity, Mr. Vaccaro. We want to make things right. The NCAA has been wronging people like me for too long. We're ready to do this. And we're going to win this."

"That's what I love to hear, Eddie!" I could hear the excitement in Mr. Vaccaro's voice. And even though he was nearly seventy years old at the time, I'm pretty sure I heard him jumping up and down in his living room.

He went on to reflect on his path to this moment. He named the other players he had contacted about joining the lawsuit. "Eddie, I tried other influential athletes, but they didn't want to take this on. They are great guys and I love them, but they didn't understand what I was talking about. They knew the NCAA was exploiting them, but they didn't feel outraged. You do. You've seen the video game, Eddie, with your own eyes. You realize what a racket this is. You know it *must* change."

Mr. Vaccaro then yelled out to his wonderful wife, Pam, "Hey, Pammie, Eddie's in!" I heard Pam cheer. And it sounded better than any cheer I'd ever heard, in any arena or on any playground.

The game was on.

CHAPTER 2

FROM ONE TO MANY

I HAD NEVER BEEN IN A LAWSUIT OR ANYTHING LIKE IT. SURE, I had a basketball agent years ago when I played in the NBA and overseas. And real estate attorneys were involved in homes that Rosa and I bought and sold. But I never needed someone to represent me in court.

So much of my life had been consumed by basketball that it didn't leave a whole lot of time for learning about the law. And, no, I'm not a civil rights leader, political activist, or social crusader. For a former NBA player who brought a historic case against the NCAA, I've lived a pretty ordinary American life.

I grew up in a middle-class home in Los Angeles County, with two loving parents, who both worked full-time jobs. Now retired, my parents love each other as much today as they did when they married nearly fifty years ago. My dad, Ed Sr., was

Here I am at three-and-a-half years old as ring bearer at my uncle's February 1976 wedding. The flower girl was Kimberly Jordan, a family friend and great niece of Jackie Robinson.

a truck driver for UPS and my mom, Madeline, was a financial clerk for a hospital in the neighborhood. Dad literally took a lunch pail to work every day and drove the big brown truck. He damn near broke his back picking up those boxes. But he'd always leave home at 5 a.m. and get home by 6 p.m., about an hour after Mom. Dad, Mom, my brother Charles, and I had dinner together every night. Our parents taught Charles and me the value of hard work and humility, and not taking anything for granted.

Ours was a pretty safe neighborhood where there were white kids, black kids, Latino kids, and Asian kids. We were by no means rich, but we weren't poor, either. But like a lot of Los Angeles neighborhoods back then, ours was always on the radar screen of one of the two main gangs, the Bloods and the Crips. For the most part, they didn't cause us trouble. And we steered clear of them the best we could. Then, sometime during my freshman year in high school, Charles came home from school and told my parents that he was given an ultimatum about being initiated into the Bloods. They didn't get his older brother, but they wanted him. My parents had heard enough. It was time to move. So, it was on to Lakewood, a neighborhood about fifteen minutes away.

Not a perfect kid by any stretch, I usually did my homework, normally followed the rules, and pretty much stuck to the routine. If you only considered where I'm from, I wouldn't seem like someone who would grow up to become the guy who launched a full-scale legal assault on a multibillion-dollar entrenched system.

• • •

Mr. Vaccaro advised me to call Michael Hausfeld, an attorney in San Francisco who had agreed to serve as lead counsel in the case. This was a big deal, Mr. Vaccaro explained, because Michael was a big deal in the legal world. He had won huge lawsuits involving victims of apartheid in South Africa and items stolen from Holocaust victims. He was truly a world-class lawyer and a champion for those who have been wronged. He had also heard a speech that Mr. Vaccaro had given at Howard University about athlete rights and was moved to reach out.

But Michael needed to hear from me—not just from Mr. Vaccaro—that I was committed. So I called him and told him I was ready to take on the NCAA. He was thrilled, and had one of his colleagues, Jon King—whom I would get to know really well—set up a meeting to talk about the case and what it would involve.

About a week later, Jon and I had lunch at a hotel in downtown Vegas. What was appealing to me from the start was that Jon treated me the way I treat my customers at Findlay. There was no pressure. There were no expectations. He kept telling me, "Ed, if you want to be part of this, great, but if you don't, or if you later on decide you want out, that's also great. Seriously." I also connected with him because he was a former Division I men's basketball player—Jon had played at Santa Clara in the late '80s. Although he played in a smaller program and was a walk-on rather than a recruit, he still understood the college athlete's perspective.

Jon explained to me the basic goal of the case: to stop the NCAA from enforcing rules that prohibit former Division I basketball and football players from compensation for the use of their names, images, and likenesses. He went on to talk about the basics of the law, how colleges claim to compete with each other but then collude when it comes to not paying former college athletes. Then he explained exactly how they use our identities—in video games, on TV, on trading cards, and the like—and how it breaks the law.

Jon made the legal arguments very understandable. He admitted that they involved fairly complicated topics under antitrust law and intellectual property law, and told me economists would be involved. But the gist of the lawsuit was actually pretty easy to understand: former college athletes have been ripped off for years, and that must end.

Jon also warned me about certain things. For starters, he said that I wouldn't make money from this case. He said that the case was about changing rules going forward, not about obtaining a financial windfall for what had happened in the past. If there would be any money for me, Jon explained, it would be a really small amount. He even said, "Ed, when you factor in your time and energy, you're going to lose money from this case. You need to weigh that." I was okay with it. My family and I were fine financially. That wasn't why we were doing this. This was about principle and fairness.

Jon also revealed that the case might last ten years or longer. *Wow, a decade.* That was long, I thought! But that was okay, too. I knew we faced a fierce opponent. Along those lines, Jon added, "The NCAA has more money than some countries. They'll hire lawyers to fight this for years. And they'll try to make you look bad, and they'll try to get you to say awful things about Sonny

Vaccaro." I still wasn't too worried. I knew I would just tell the truth and everything would be fine.

Then Jon got to a topic that did cause me concern. "Ed," he warned, "you haven't been on *SportsCenter* in a long time, but you will be after this case is filed—and they might not like you anymore." Jon also stressed that media is different than it was in the '90s, with Facebook and everything being online. "It's a lot easier to attack someone and do so anonymously," Jon emphasized. "And you're going to get a lot of blowback."

That prophecy would prove true. But as I'll explain later, I was okay with getting attacked—I've played hoops in some pretty hostile places and heard some awful things said to me by angry fans. It was what my family might hear and how it would impact their lives that concerned me. It still does to this day.

Jon also warned me that the path from filing the lawsuit to the actual trial would not be a straight one. That certainly proved true. I looked at it this way: It's like running up a basketball court while on offense. You almost never get to the hoop without having to overcome some obstacles along the way. There are defensive players who harass you for the ball. They poke. They prod. They rip. Some of them are really good at it. Then there are the refs. Occasionally they make good calls. Occasionally they don't. Either way, they slow you down. And then there's the possibility of falling or tripping while running, or—as I know too well—landing awkwardly after a jump. There are so many ways you and your teammates can get hurt as you travel across the ninety-four feet that separate the two baskets.

There are also interruptions. Your coach might unexpectedly change the play and yell out a new one. You might suddenly see an opening to score and alter your movement to pursue it, only to see that opening close just as quickly as it came. Even a fan can cause a delay. It's rare, but people in the stands have been known to throw objects onto the court.

There are all sorts of hurdles before you score. Some of them appear more often than others. Some of them are more predictable than not. But you almost never go directly from one end of the court to the hoop at the other end.

So the fact that our lawsuit required adjustments along the way was not unfamiliar territory for me.

And adjustments would occur early on.

Less than a year after I sued in the US District Court for the Northern District of California in 2009, the judge assigned to our case, Judge Claudia Wilken, combined our case with a similar one brought by former University of Arizona quarterback Sam Keller. Both Sam and I argued that the NCAA couldn't own our intellectual property rights forever, and we were both outraged by the video games and other merchandise that feature former players. By bringing us together, our cases became stronger.

Another positive change occurred when several legendary players joined my lawsuit as named plaintiffs. Within that first year, Harry Flournoy and David Lattin—teammates on the 1966 Texas Western University team that became the first college team to win the NCAA basketball tournament with an all-black starting lineup—said they wanted in. And then two of the best players of all time, Oscar Robertson and Bill Russell, came on board. As the longest-serving president of the National Basketball Players Association, Oscar Robertson had already blazed a trail with the 1976 Oscar Robertson Rule, which helped NBA players become the first professional athletes to achieve free agency. Bill Russell, in addition to his eleven championship rings with the Boston Celtics, was an outspoken voice on civil rights matters in the mid-1960s, at a time when professional athletes were strongly discouraged from speaking out on social issues.

The case became truly a cause for justice. And it was a cause that people with serious and respected reputations were willing to put their names on. I was honored to lead it.

There were a couple of changes to the lawsuit that gave me pause, however.

In 2012 Michael Hausfeld called me and said that he wanted to expand the lawsuit. He proposed that we sue over the use of both former *and* current players' names, images, and likenesses. As Michael explained it, the legal arguments for paying former players also held true for current ones. Plus, the case would have a greater impact if current players were included: we could go after the billions of dollars of live television money from tournament broadcasts. Michael also told me that he and the other lawyers were in touch with current players who were very interested in joining.

I'd be lying if I said I had no concerns.

When I started the lawsuit in 2009, it had nothing to do with college athletes getting paid or going after revenue from live TV broadcasts. At the time, those seemed like totally different topics from EA Sports and the NCAA making money from video games that used my identity long after I had finished college. That was the harmful action I wanted remedied, not only for me but also for other former players who were featured in those games. And though I was less offended by rebroadcasts of my old UCLA games on ESPN and by various merchandise sales, I still objected to them because they similarly generated money through the work and identities of former players. My lawsuit was really about former players like myself being duped by the NCAA and companies that made video games, rebroadcasts, and merchandise using our names, images, and likenesses.

I wasn't interested in a larger lawsuit that would center on kids currently in college. I was turning forty years old in 2012 and had teenage children. I identified with other former players who were like me—guys who had long since played and who were working jobs and providing for their families. Along those lines, I liked the fact that no one could say that our scholarships or "free educations" served as the compensation for our names, images, and likenesses. Those scholarships had long since run out and our formal education was long since over. The NCAA and EA profiting from our former fame had nothing to do with education or scholarships. It was simply theft. Players currently on scholarships and receiving educations? They seemed like a very different group from the group that I saw myself in.

And to be honest, the idea of becoming the plaintiff on behalf of seventeen-year-olds seemed kind of out of place. If I were coming out of high school and some old dude had a fight against the NCAA, I probably wouldn't have paid attention to it and I'd sure be reluctant to become part of it. Plus, I didn't want to infringe on their careers and what they were trying to accomplish. I would never ask current athletes to join me. They had to find that from within. They had to find their own fighters.

An expanded lawsuit might have even further implications regarding "amateur" sports. Would I be comfortable with them? If it succeeded, would the lawsuit mean that sports agents would represent college athletes? Would agents be walking around on campus? How exactly would all that work?

I had a serious conversation with Michael Hausfeld and Mr. Vaccaro about the expansion. "What you guys are telling me is a different can of worms," I told them. "I really don't want to tackle this beast. This isn't my fight. I don't want to pick on those dudes." I told them they had to convince me.

And they did. They showed me how much money the NCAA and colleges were making off current players. They also explained a system without sports agents strolling through campus, but instead with a national trade association that negotiates on behalf of college athletes and does so ethically and transparently. The goal would be basic fairness, not making the star point guard or quarterback rich.

Michael and Mr. Vaccaro also reminded me to think back

on when I was in college and the conversations I had with teammates. I remember how frustrated we all felt. But we knew that we were on scholarship and so talking out of turn was risky. In a lot of ways we felt voiceless. "Nothing's changed, Ed," Michael remarked. "Except the system is worse now than it was when you played. And it's only going to worsen unless we do something about it. We've got to change the rules."

Michael was right. This was not just a fight about video games, trading cards, and T-shirts that steal identities. It was a fight about changing the system that made it so easy for that theft to take place. And it was theft that happened from the moment you walked on campus and continued until the day you passed away many years later. They put you on TV, brochures, and websites. Your name appears on replica jerseys that sell for over a hundred dollars. And you can't get a dime from any of it because when you were seventeen years old you somehow waived away your rights, permanently and forever, as a condition of NCAA eligibility and thus a condition of getting a college scholarship and affording school.

That's not "amateurism." That's exploitation.

So, this was a turning point for me based on new information and different perspectives. When the NCAA deposed me in 2011, I drew a line between current athletes and former ones. I was in a different place in my life at that time. I honestly hadn't considered whether the line between current and former college players is solid, dotted, or flat-out imaginary. The more I learned about the economics of college sports and the real intentions of NCAA rules, the more I realized there is no line. College sports have become pro sports, just dressed up as something different, something that allows it to use athletes' names, images, and likenesses freely. But the line between college and postcollege isn't there. The NCAA sets the value they're willing to pay for former *and* current players' names, images, and likenesses at zero dollars.

It's not about whether you're in school or out of school. It's about whether you're getting ripped off.

There could have been one case against the NCAA and EA on behalf of former players and a second case on behalf of current players. But there was more strength if they were joined together in one powerful lawsuit. The more I recognized that the underlying rules impacted both groups, the more I knew the cases should be linked. And I wanted my name to be the name on the case that would redesign this entire system.

• • •

The scope of the lawsuit expanded, and there was a second significant change in the litigation that troubled me. Unlike the first one, this one still disappoints me.

I could talk to Jon King in a different way than I could talk with the other lawyers. He would walk me through details and helped me understand core strategies and their pros and cons. He had this knack for explaining complicated points in straightforward ways. But then, just like that, Jon left the case. I was never told why Michael fired Jon. I still don't know to this day. Jon sent me a gracious email saying that he wasn't going to be part of the case anymore, and he expressed gratitude for working with me. Then I read internet stories suggesting that he had been forced out in a power struggle. At that point I was like, *What the heck is happening here?*

No one had given me a heads up about what was going to happen and no one explained to me why it happened—and I was the plaintiff. Sure, I was told that lawyers come and go during litigations and not to be alarmed. I understand that teams of lawyers change over the years, just like teams of athletes change over time. But it was obvious to me that there were other things going on. As time went on, I heard that there were some differences between Jon and Michael and that those differences had been building up over the years. But I never heard any specifics.

Don't get me wrong: my lawyers were awesome. Other than the reason for Jon's departure, my lawyers always kept me informed about developments. I just didn't have the same rapport with Michael that I had with Jon. And Michael was the boss and always pretty busy.

Not too long thereafter, Sathya Gosselin joined the legal team and became my contact person. Next man up, as the New England Patriots like to say. Sathya was a younger guy, in his early thirties. He didn't try to be Jon King 2.0. He was just himself. The biggest problem that coaches and mentors have as far as taking over that role is that they try to be the person they are replacing. Sathya never did that. He stayed genuine and I respected that. He was always available when I called. He always kept me in the loop, and he and I eventually became really good friends.

There were bumps in the road and some unexpected turns during the litigation. But we retained possession of the ball with the opportunity to put the NCAA on trial.

CHAPTER 3

TRUST THE PROCESS

FROM THE DAY WE FILED THE LAWSUIT, I KNEW YEARS WOULD pass before there would be an actual trial. My lawyers—Jon King, Michael Hausfeld, and, later, Sathya Gosselin—were upfront about that. They cautioned me that lawsuits sometimes take years to play out, especially complex and groundbreaking ones like ours. Sure enough, seven years later our case was still going on.

We would first have to be certified as a class action, so that I could sue on behalf of others. That would require my lawyers showing that my "legal injury"—being depicted in video games and classic TV broadcasts without my permission—was a similar kind of injury to those suffered by other former players. It obviously was. Then we'd have to defeat various NCAA and EA motions to have the case dismissed.

At times I felt like I had enrolled in law school! The legal world really has its own language. Just like when you live in a foreign country, I picked up a few words here and there. But from the get-go, my lawyers assured me that they would respect my time and do everything possible not to interfere with my day-to-day life. The legal stuff was their job, not mine. And that basically proved true. I was updated regularly on the case and I'd ask questions, but otherwise I continued to live my life as I had before.

That said, my lawyers warned me that I'd be needed for one critical part of pretrial. At some point, NCAA attorneys would "depose" me. This would be in person and face-to-face. I had heard of depositions from watching movies and TV shows, but I honestly didn't know their purpose or process. As I discovered, both sides use depositions to make witnesses testify under oath long before the trial. Depositions don't involve the judge and they don't happen in court. Instead, they take place at the law firm of one of the lawyers—if it's the office of your attorney, it's kind of like your home court. And a deposition reporter is there to create a record. Call him the scorekeeper.

Depositions are sort of like games. One side's lawyer asks tough questions to the other side's witness in hopes that the witness will admit fault or reveal some damaging info. Looking back, depositions helped our side immensely. NCAA and Electronic Arts executives admitted to my lawyers that they intended to make video games based on real players and that the NCAA would not share the profits with the players. Those admissions played a major role in EA wanting to settle with us before the trial.

I felt really nervous as the day of my deposition approached. Up until that point, I hadn't spoken with "the other side." I had no interaction with NCAA attorneys and the closest I had ever been to NCAA President Mark Emmert was when he appeared on my living room TV preaching the false cult of amateurism.

The Monday before my deposition I met with Michael Hausfeld at his office in San Francisco. It almost felt fitting that it was Halloween 2011. I told Michael that I was worried about how I should appear and sound during the deposition. Do I need to seem very serious or can I be more relaxed? Do I need to have everything from our case researched? Am I going to be hit with questions about the law? Basically, I asked Michael, "Can I be me or do I need to go as someone else?"

Michael made it clear that I was to be the same old Ed during the deposition. "Ed, I want you to feel relaxed and I want you to tell the truth. And don't worry about the questions being asked—you'll get a lot of them and they'll be about all sorts of things. Worry instead about how you answer them. Think of it like having a conversation."

Michael gave me one stern warning: "Whatever happens, don't be confrontational. Just be you. Be as calm as possible."

Michael diffused some of the tension I was feeling, but I still felt nervous the next day. This was my first deposition. My first legal appearance. My first lawsuit. Call it whatever you want. I had never put my hand on the Bible and sworn to God before. All of this was new to me. When I arrived at Michael's law firm, my palms were sweaty, my stomach turned upside down. I don't remember even my biggest basketball games making me feel like this.

There was, though, another day in my life where I felt that kind of anxiety: June 28, 1995. For the basketball world, that was the day of the 1995 NBA draft.

• • •

Winning an NCAA championship may be a one-night event, but it has an aftermath. And that aftermath included a big buildup to the stress I felt on June 28, 1995. There was one transition after the next. It began by UCLA asking my teammates and me to come back to campus several times after classes were over in '95 for championship ceremonies and celebrations. There were award banquets, parties, dinners with alumni—you name it.

There were TV show appearances, too. Talk about being a fish out of water! For example, Tyus Edney and I appeared on an episode of *Hope & Gloria*. You may not remember the show. It was a '90s sitcom about a TV producer, played by Cynthia Stevenson, and her beautician neighbor, played by Jessica Lundy. Alan Thicke also starred. Anyway, I met Thicke and Burt Reynolds, who was guest-starring in an episode. It was so much fun. I had to memorize lines and dance to choreography—and I'm not a dancer! I've always wanted to be an actor, so this was a real treat. I was starstruck by meeting these actors, but also stunned by how much *they* thought they were around celebrities. It was just Tyus and me!

We also did the late-night show circuit, including *The Tonight Show with Jay Leno*. I met Jay backstage while we were conducting a walk-through with the producer. Jay saw us and was holding the cover of *Sports Illustrated* with me on it at the time. I had not seen the cover yet. Pointing at the cover, he said, in his Boston accent, "Where's this guy? I want to meet him!"

My teammates were like, "Man, you got the cover! Nice!"

I just stood there. I had chills going up and down my spine. *I'm on the cover of* Sports Illustrated. *And I'm finding out about it from Jay Leno, who wants to meet me.*

So, our NCAA championship was a celebration for me, but also for the university and for everyone associated with it. And I wasn't quite ready to leave UCLA.

A lot of my life was still at UCLA, and I still enjoyed living in Los Angeles. Rosa felt the same way. She was co-owner of a clothing and accessory boutique in Manhattan Beach and worked there part-time. Her business was thriving—she has a real gift for recognizing fashion trends and the business smarts to capitalize on those trends before her competitors. Both of our parents lived nearby and they loved to visit Aaron, our son. It was a place where we felt at home.

We also secured some spending money when I signed a five-year endorsement deal with Nike. It was designed to pay me $375,000 each year for five years, but I would only collect if I remained on an NBA roster. It instantly infused us with the kind of money we had not seen before.

You might say that during the spring and summer of 1995 I never quite left UCLA and its surroundings. I knew my life was changing, but it's hard to walk away from what was a really special time.

While my ties to LA kept me there, I had a big international trip in June. Destination: Toronto. I had an NBA draft to attend, and it would be at the SkyDome.

The NBA draft takes place on one night, but it's really a five-day affair for the entire family. Rosa, Mom, Dad, Charles, my grandparents, and I all made the cross-country and international flight from Los Angeles to Toronto to take part in one of the most memorable experiences of my life.

The NBA rolls out the red carpet for the soon-to-be drafted players once they arrive. For example, the league took us out for some local enjoyment, like a cruise around Niagara Falls and a laser tag competition. All the guys got to know each other well, which for me was a new experience. You see, I usually didn't fraternize with the guys I played against. That was how I kept my edge. If you and I were friends, it would be harder for me to beat you on the court. So I wouldn't become your friend in the first place. I know that may sound harsh and, nowadays, pretty strange, too. If you go on Instagram this afternoon, you'll probably see NBA players on rival teams liking each other's posts as though they're best buddies. I may come across like an old man here, but back in my day that kind of stuff wasn't cool at all.

I approached my competitors with Larry Bird and Magic Johnson in mind. Whenever Bird and Magic interacted on the court, it was pure hostility. They genuinely disliked one another and admitted as much. Their animosity began in college, when Magic's Michigan State Spartans defeated Bird's Indiana State Sycamores in the 1979 NCAA title game. Their rivalry continued into the NBA and helped make for some incredible NBA finals between the Celtics and the Lakers. As a Lakers fan I watched that intensity up close. It made an impression on me as to how basketball should be played.

Bird and Magic were frosty off the court, too. They went about their separate ways. When that wasn't possible, like at All-Star game parties and other events attended by NBA stars, they avoided talking to each other. This was all by design. They were true competitors. I love that. That kind of distant approach gave Bird and Magic an edge that—along with Hall-of-Fame-worthy talent and a dogged work ethic—made them two of the best players of all time.

I adopted that same approach. When I was off the court, I went about my separate way. I didn't grab beers with the guy I was going to match up against next week. I didn't laugh it up with players I might face in the postseason. I preserved my advantage at all costs. I remember really disliking Damon Stoudamire, who was a terrific point guard at the University of Arizona. Don't get me wrong—my man could ball and I totally respected his game. But I couldn't stand the team's trash talking and I thought that was kind of arrogant. I just didn't like it. They probably thought the exact same thing about me.

But what happened when I spent some time with Damon

before the draft? The dude was a great guy, and we are friends to this day. Same goes for Corliss Williamson, who was the star of the University of Arkansas team that we defeated in the NCAA title game a few months prior. I didn't know how he would take to me and I'm sure the feeling was mutual. He struggled in the title game so I kind of wondered if he would resent me. But instead we hit it off. Corliss had snakes for pets at the time and in Los Angeles that's unheard of—we don't do that stuff in LA—he was a different cat, but we broke bread and laughed.

So, then came draft day: June 28, 1995. I would have a very good seat for it. The NBA had invited me to the "green room," which isn't actually a room. It's more about proximity to the stage and prestige—a group of tables positioned in front of the podium where the NBA commissioner announces a team's draft selection. It's a major honor to get invited. Only the players who are expected to be among the first fifteen picks snag invites. Each of those players gets his own table for his family and friends. Other players only attend by being in the audience with everyone else.

Green room tables were also the focus of TNT's television broadcast. The camera zooms in on the moms, dads, grandparents, and girlfriends—anyone sitting at the table with the player—to see if their faces show some kind of noteworthy emotion.

Unfortunately, in every draft there is some guy sitting in the green room who isn't drafted as highly as expected. He and his family sit anxiously, made to feel worse by knowing the camera is on them. Meanwhile, people at home watch him and his family become more disappointed and dejected as the night marches on.

I was pretty certain that wouldn't be me. However, I was concerned about how teams might have evaluated my knee, which I had injured in 1990, and whether they were paranoid about it. I felt great physically. For three years I had been able to play without any problems or limitations—heck, I played all forty minutes in the championship game and was the only player on either the Bruins or Razorbacks to do so.

But teams wanted to know if I could withstand an eighty-two-game NBA season. And so every team that evaluated me spent a lot of time looking at my knee and examining it. I'll tell you later about my knee injury, but for now let's just say I went for a dunk in a scrimmage and landed the wrong way—and ended up with a dead man's Achilles tendon being placed in my knee. Teams would have one doctor look at my knee and then they would have another one do the same. Rinse and repeat.

At times I felt like I was auditioning my health as much as my basketball skills. It was frustrating because I thought the knee injury was a thing of the past. It had happened years ago, and there I was in 1995 having to answer questions about it. It seemed unfair that one silly dunk in a meaningless scrimmage would take on more significance than anything else in my basketball life. On the other hand, I understood where teams were coming from. They have only one shot to get it right. If a general manager selects the wrong player and a player he passed on becomes an NBA star, that GM will be blamed and could even be fired. The stakes are high.

With mixed feelings, for sure, I felt pretty certain I would be picked in the top ten. So I wanted to look the part. I wanted to look handsome. You see, when I was growing up, my mom would call me "Handsome." If there was ever a night that I wanted to live up to that nickname, it was draft night. I wanted to make my mom proud.

I also wanted to look dignified. I knew that players occasionally wore flashy, almost outrageous suits to the NBA draft. I didn't want to do that. For one, I didn't want people years later showing a photo of me in a crazy suit and laughing not with me but *at* me. I'm also a pretty conservative guy at heart. I wanted a distinguished look that would set the tone that I was becoming a professional and was serious about it.

I wore a three-piece suit that was grayish-blue—they call it cadet blue—and it looked sharp. Pleated pants. White socks. Dotted red tie. Tailor made. The whole shebang. I still have it in my closet. I had picked it about a month earlier, when I attended the NBA draft combine, a showcase for draft-eligible players and an opportunity to meet with teams. There was a tailor there who showed soon-to-be draftees like me a huge book of fabrics and colors. The book was gigantic. It was bigger than any Bible I've seen!

At the draft, I sat with Rosa, my parents, my grandparents, Charles, and my agent, Arn Tellem. We were all nervous. I was about to find out where I would spend the next several years of my life. We sat patiently and watched how the evening would unfold. I didn't expect to go among the first four picks and I indeed did not.

Then the draft turned to my expected range—picks five to ten.

The Timberwolves, however, picked Kevin Garnett at number five and the Grizzlies then selected Bryant Reeves number six. I was a little bit disappointed to see that. I thought I had a decent shot to be picked by one of those teams. But I also knew that Garnett was quickly moving up teams' draft boards. They realized that although Garnett was straight out of high school, he was a bona fide star in the making. And he certainly turned out to be one. Reeves, who had dominated at the University of Oklahoma, stood a legit seven feet tall and wasn't lacking in muscle. They didn't call him "Big Country" for nothing. So, I understood those picks.

Then the Raptors were up. This was a special night for that team. The Raptors were brand new. They were an expansion team, and making their first-ever draft pick. The crowd of twenty-one thousand people, many of whom were from Toronto or the surrounding area, started cheering. This was their moment.

They also started chanting three words that definitely caught my attention.

"WE WANT ED!" "WE WANT ED!" "WE WANT ED!"

I was laughing and loving it. My whole table was digging it. Some of the fans were holding signs that just said ED. It was an honor to see a fan base—even if it was brand-spanking new—speak out for me. They weren't worried about my knee.

But while Raptors fans wanted me, the TNT TV crew didn't walk over to my table. This was an ominous sign.

Back then, there were two ways to find out whether a team had drafted you. You could wait to hear if Commissioner David Stern called your name. Or you could pay attention to a revealing hint that took place moments before he spoke. The TNT camera crew would quietly walk over and position themselves next to the table of the player whose name Stern would call about thirty seconds later. They did this so they could get their cameras on the facial reactions of the player and his family members right as Stern announced his name. In other words, the TV people knew before you did if you were picked.

And remember, in 1995, there were no texts and emails. You couldn't go on Twitter and read a "Wojbomb" from Adrian Wojnarowski about where everyone was going in the draft. I think that guy knows who is going to get drafted before even the teams do! Back then, it was either wait for Stern to say your name or watch the whereabouts of the TNT cameramen.

With the Raptors on the board, I looked for the cameramen…

…creeping over to the table of Damon Stoudamire.

And then the commissioner started walking over to the podium. I heard the audience again chant, "WE WANT ED! WE WANT ED!"

They would not be getting Ed.

"With the seventh pick in the 1995 NBA draft—their first draft and their first pick—the Toronto Raptors select Damon Stoudamire from the University of Arizona."

And then the chorus of boos began. It continued even as Damon walked toward the podium to be greeted by the commissioner. I felt bad for Damon—he didn't deserve that. Neither did his family. You're not supposed to be booed on what should be the night of your basketball life.

Damon would have the last laugh, though. He won the NBA's Rookie of the Year Award and went on to a long and successful NBA career. He retired from the NBA at age thirty-five in 2008, which was eleven years after I played my last NBA game.

So, I didn't end up with the Raptors. But I thought that there was a good chance the Trailblazers, which had the eighth pick, would take me. And, man, Portland would have been a great fit for my Californian life.

"With the eighth pick in the 1995 NBA draft, the Portland Trailblazers select Shawn Respert from Michigan State University."

Okay, so cross Portland off the list. Now my heart is pumping. And I later found out from people who were watching the draft at home that the TNT hosts—Ernie Johnson, Hubie Brown, and Rick Pitino—were beginning to speculate at that time that I was "falling" due to concerns about my knee. Glad I didn't know it at the time.

For his part, Brown—who I had never met and I'm not sure had ever seen me play in person—said on the air, "Everything is going to come down to the doctors for a particular team in regard to Ed O'Bannon, because the talent is there. It's whether or not the doctors will allow a team or suggest to a team that they should gamble and take him with the pick."

Gamble?

I get that I had a knee injury, but man, it was four years

earlier and I had clearly recovered from it. I didn't win the John Wooden Award on one knee!

The anxiety was really starting to kick in. Damn, would I be *that guy* who drops? I had been so confident before the draft started that I wouldn't be him. But thoughts started to cross my mind. How low could I go?

Well, the Nets were up next with the ninth pick. Their general manager, Willis Reed, would be making the selection. Reed is a legendary figure in basketball and someone whom I admire greatly. He played his college ball in the early '60s at Grambling State University, a historically black college, and he became a superstar forward for the New York Knicks. "The Captain," as he was called, was voted one of the fifty greatest players in NBA history. And he is rightfully enshrined in the Basketball Hall of Fame. We were about the same height and I could see some similarities in our games.

I had met Reed for the first time in February of that year. He was scouting our game against the University of California at Harmon Gym in Berkeley. I impressed Reed in more ways than one that evening. On the court, I was on fire. I tied Reggie Miller's UCLA school record by making seven 3-pointers. I did so efficiently, too, hitting seven of my nine 3-point attempts. I finished the game with 27 points. It was one of my best games of the season.

After the game ended, my teammates and I started walking toward the locker room. It was more crowded than usual, with a lot of people on the floor. It seemed security wasn't doing much crowd control. Anyway, as I was trying to get through the crowd, several people stopped me to congratulate me on tying Miller's record. Getting to where I needed to go was taking some time. I then noticed two young women who were walking in my direction. They were making eye contact. In the interest of full disclosure, they were gorgeous—they were dime pieces. When they reached me, they told me how impressed they were by how I played in the game. They then asked me questions about playing and made other chit-chat.

It was flattering, and part of the life of a basketball player. There is no shortage of attractive young women who pay you compliments. The groupies find you after games. They find you in restaurants and bars. They track you down in hotel lobbies and at charity events. They even approach you while you're moving a cart around a supermarket. Sometimes they don't care if your wife is standing right beside you and is obviously your wife. It's like they are under a spell because you're a basketball star. Some players who aren't particularly skilled at self-control can get into a lot of trouble when they operate in this space. They can be so remarkably disciplined at sports as to become world-class athletes, yet when it comes to personal conduct, they prove quite vulnerable to temptation.

Anyway, as these young women were asking me questions, Willis Reed was standing next to me wanting to chat. I had absolutely no idea he was there. I then felt a person tap me on the shoulder, which is not a common occurrence given that I'm six foot eight. It's usually a sign that a fellow basketball player is trying to get my attention.

I turned around and looked right at Willis Reed. As I began to smile, Reed introduced himself, as if I didn't know who he was. He needed no introduction to me. He didn't stop to talk, though. Instead, he just said, "Wonderful game, young man," and kept walking. The two women then started asking me more questions. I didn't make anything of it at the time.

Then in June, a few weeks before the draft, I worked out with the Nets. Reed came to see me and reintroduced himself. "Ed, I don't know if you recall, but we met briefly in Berkeley."

"I do remember that, sir. It was an honor to meet you; I've always admired your game and have tried to learn from it."

"Well, I would have talked to you more in Berkeley," Reed explained, "but I didn't want to interrupt your conversation. From my eyes you were busy." He smiled and let out a hearty laugh. I chuckled too, and replied, "Man, you are Willis Reed— who wouldn't want to talk to you??!!" It was a great way to break the ice and I felt a bond with him.

So back at the draft, there I was, sitting in the SkyDome wondering if Willis Reed thought the bond was strong enough to draft me. There were a lot of good players left on the board. And many of them, like me, played forward. Corliss Williamson. Theo Ratliff. Kurt Thomas. Gary Trent. It was no sure thing that Reed thought more of me than those guys.

As I was contemplating Reed's choice, I saw a man holding a camera and another man in front of him quickly walking toward my table. It was the TNT crew.

Yes. Finally. I can breathe.

"With the ninth pick in the 1995 NBA draft," Stern announced in his distinctive New York accent, "the New Jersey Nets select Ed O'Bannon from UCLA."

I kept my cool and stood up. No smiling, at least not for the first few seconds. I was turning pro, after all. Time to put my serious face on. But everyone else at my table smiled, cheered, or cried in joy. I first leaned over to kiss Rosa, and then my mom and grandma. My serious face was gone—I was smiling wide at that point! I hugged my dad and shook his hand firmly. And then, last but not least, I hugged Charles. I had saved the biggest hug for my brother. He knew, more than anyone, how hard it was for me to get to this point. And there I was. Lottery pick in the NBA draft.

I then started my walk up to the podium. But before I made it far, my dad grabbed me and gave me another hug—a bear hug. He had played wide receiver at UCLA in the early '70s but didn't make it to the NFL. He understood the long odds of going from

I traveled the road
to the NBA Draft with
my brother by my side
the whole way.

My official Draft Day
photo. (Courtesy of
Brooklyn Sports &
Entertainment)

college sports to pro sports. He whispered in my ear, "You did it, son." He was so proud. I looked over to my mom and she had tears welling in her eyes.

Man, I was so full of emotion at that point, but I needed to keep it together. I started to walk toward the podium. An attendant handed me a New Jersey Nets cap. I fixed the bill—I don't do the straight bill on a cap, it has to be curved—and I put it on, real tight. No way was it going to fall off.

I then adjusted my suit to make sure it looked neat, and began to walk up the steps toward the stage.

The Toronto crowd was cheering louder for me than any other player picked so far, including even the guy picked by the Raptors. I almost felt like I was back at the Pauley Pavilion with thousands of Bruins fans watching and applauding.

Later on, I watched the reaction of the TV guys as this was all happening. And I loved it. "This young man is a big-time winner," Rick Pitino said. "A big-time competitor, and he's from a great family." Unlike Hubie Brown, I knew Pitino had actually seen me play in person. I had put up twenty-six points against his University of Kentucky Wildcats team the previous November. He knew the kind of player I was. He knew that I could ball. And, maybe most importantly, he saw firsthand that my repaired knee didn't impede my play at all.

When I got to the top of the stage of the SkyDome I looked over and saw Commissioner Stern, who smiled at me. This is a man who never really smiles, yet there he was doing just that.

At that point it got surreal. I don't even remember walking over to the commissioner. I felt like I was gliding across the stage to him. It reminded me of what Spike Lee does in all of his films. There's always a scene where people glide. It's called the dolly shot. There's a camera in front of the actor and another camera right above him. Together the two cameras give the illusion of the actor floating over the ground, almost like he is in his own dimension and in control of his own world. It's a beautiful thing.

When I arrived at the podium, I shook the commissioner's hand. He congratulated me and pointed me in the direction of the photographer for an official photograph of the two of us.

I was on cloud nine. This was really happening.

I moved to the side of the stage, where Craig Sager from TNT would interview me. Until Craig passed away in 2016 after a long battle with leukemia, it had long been a rite of passage for players at the draft to get interviewed by the TV man with the flashy suits. There was only one Craig Sager. The man was a legend.

Craig first asked me about the incredible run I'd been on, between winning the national championship and now a top-ten pick. I thanked the Lord for it and I still do. Craig's second question wasn't as favorable. He asked about other NBA teams "staying away" from me because of "the arthritis in the knee," and he wanted to know what doctors had told me about the "durability" of playing an eighty-two-game season. I wasn't offended by the question—as a broadcaster and journalist, Craig had to ask me about my knee or he wasn't doing his job. But I still didn't like how the question implied that I was damaged goods.

Part of me wanted to tell Craig, *"Look, dude, I just played three long seasons with post-tournament play. I led my team in games and minutes played—by quite a bit, too. I crashed the boards and led the team in rebounding. I dove for the ball. I banged for space underneath the hoop. I think I'm okay, don't you?"* But my parents taught me to be graceful and diplomatic even under the most stressful of situations, and that's how I acted in the interview.

So, I politely responded to Craig's question by saying that for every NBA rookie—whether he's from college or high school—there's an adjustment period to playing an eighty-two-game season. I also emphasized that my knee was fine and that the doctors had looked at it and given their thumbs-up. Then I said, "Look at the game films. My legs are stronger than ever."

After the TNT interview I went backstage and shook hands with a lot of people. There were other media interviews to attend to as well. But at one point I looked over to the SkyDome's video board and saw my brother, who was a rising junior at UCLA, doing his own interview on TNT. He was as cool as a cucumber and the only man in the building wearing sunglasses!

We got back to our hotel room and ordered up delicious food and drinks and celebrated the night away. Everything was real light. All of the jokes were funny, all of the stories were interesting. It was really a hell of a summer—from winning a national championship on April 3 and celebrating with my teammates to signing with Nike and now being a lottery pick in the NBA draft. This was the high time of my life and career.

• • •

Anxiety had turned into elation on draft day, June 28, 1995. And that was because I had done right by my teammates and coaches. I needed to remember that lesson on "deposition day," November 1, 2011, when Michael brought me into that conference room with the NCAA awaiting.

I was in the right and had nothing to fear from the NCAA.

I sat at an oval table. I was on one side with my lawyers.

I remember looking across as the NCAA attorneys sat there, comfortably. Well dressed. Confident. Smug. Self-assured. You get my drift.

They looked at me with polite smiles, but in my mind, they were like prizefighters. They wanted to feel me out and see how I'd respond to different kinds of questions—and then try to pummel me once I showed a weak spot.

Michael made me aware of the camera directed right at me. I was sworn in and asked to repeat, "I swear by the Almighty God that the evidence I shall give shall be the truth, the whole truth, and nothing but the truth."

If this were a basketball game, then the referee had just tossed up the ball for the tip-off.

It was time to get real.

The NCAA lawyer who would be asking me questions introduced himself as Gregory Curtner. He was an older, gray-haired fellow with a Midwestern accent. Curtner made it clear from the outset what he hoped to accomplish: get me to say that I had been paid to bring the lawsuit and that I was a naïve pawn for Mr. Vaccaro.

I'm biased here, but Curtner failed badly.

First off, I told Curtner point-blank that I hadn't been paid to bring the lawsuit and that I wasn't going to be paid, either. I sensed that he and the other NCAA attorneys were shocked, annoyed really, to hear my answers—almost like they had assumed I was going to say, "Yes, I've been paid, but…" If I had been paid, the deposition would have gone in a completely different direction and featured a completely different dialogue. But that's not what happened.

To be honest, while Curtner kept hammering me with questions about all of the different ways that I could have been paid—cash payments, wired money, gifts, you name it—it crossed my mind, *Well, damn, I could have gotten paid for this?* But getting paid was never part of it. Nothing was ever offered to me. And I never asked, either.

Curtner also aggressively asked me questions about my interactions with Mr. and Mrs. Vaccaro from way back in high school. Keep in mind, more than twenty years had passed since those days. Curtner kept badgering me to remember conversations I had had with the Vaccaros during the Nike camps.

"Did he ever pay you, Mr. O'Bannon?"

"Absolutely not."

"Did Mr. Vaccaro convince you to bring this lawsuit, Mr. O'Bannon?"

"No, sir. I brought this lawsuit because I've been wronged and so have others."

I was surprised Curtner had so many questions about the Vaccaros and their supposed intentions. The case was about me and other former players. It was not about the Vaccaros.

I also found Curtner's line of questioning to be personally offensive. I say that for two reasons. First, Curtner depicted Mr. Vaccaro as a villain in the sports world. This was completely untrue. I had known Mr. and Mrs. Vaccaro for more than two decades. These were good souls. Sure, Mr. Vaccaro wanted to see college athletes compensated for their labor and how their identities are used. Why, again, is that a bad thing? Second, Curtner implied that Mr. Vaccaro was using me as a puppet and that I didn't really know what I was doing. Sorry, that's just wrong and condescending—I knew exactly what this case was about and I knew exactly the place where I was coming from. These issues had been on my mind for more than two decades.

My case was for the greater good and for the college athlete. My decision to sue was 100 percent my decision. To the extent that that decision involved other people, they were Rosa and our kids—not the Vaccaros, in spite of the mutual respect we had for each other.

While Curtner was talking, I was literally thinking, *Man, do you not understand what this is all about and who's standing up here? Do you not get it?* To be honest, Curtner reflected the core problem with NCAA officials: they underestimate the intelligence and awareness of the athletes that they try to regulate. We're not the dumb jocks they think we are.

Curtner did try to trip me up at one point toward the end

of the deposition, which took several hours. He asked me about comments I had made back in March 2010 to Steve Kanigher, a reporter from the *Las Vegas Sun*. I had forgotten about that story, as I had done a bunch of interviews in 2010 about the case. Well, Kanigher had come out to see me at Findlay. In his article, I'm quoted extensively. I talk at length about the corruptness of the NCAA in taking advantage of players and how college athletes and former college athletes must stand up to the NCAA.

Along those lines, I'm quoted in the story as saying I had never been paid to appear in video games or in ESPN Classic rebroadcasts of my UCLA games—even though I'm still paid royalties for appearing as myself in TV shows, those 1995 post–NCAA championship appearances on *Hope & Gloria*, *Diagnosis Murder*, and *Unhappily Ever After*. I even have an IMDB page. I earn very little from those appearances, but what's important is *that* I'm paid, not how much I'm paid. The Screen Actors Guild–American Federation of Television and Radio Artists labor union ensures that is the case. Why, then, am I paid for rebroadcasts of my sitcom appearances from the '90s but not rebroadcasts of my NCAA appearances from the '90s? So-called amateurism in action, you might say.

Anyway, in Kanigher's article, I'm also quoted as saying, "Maybe athletes shouldn't get paid while they're in school. I understand that. They're on scholarship. But once we leave, why can't we take our likeness?'" Curtner confronted me about that statement and tried to get me to say that I don't think college athletes should be paid for anything. I actually didn't recall ever saying what he read back to me. I still don't to this day. I'm not saying Kanigher misquoted me, as other portions of his story seem right, more or less. But I literally have no recollection of ever saying those words or saying anything about athletes being paid while in school.

Curtner was unrelenting, finally asking me, "I mean, this

is your—an accurate statement of your belief, is it not, sir, that college sports should remain amateur and that college athletes shouldn't get paid while they're in school?" By that point I had grown tired of Curtner asking the same question in different ways. So I responded, "Yeah, I think so." Curtner then asked for a break. I suppose he got what he wanted.

Remember, at the time, our case was only about former players. In 2012—as I've described—that would change, but during my deposition in 2011 and while I interviewed with Kanigher in 2010, our case was about the use of *former* players' names, images, and likenesses. I therefore didn't quite understand the relevance of his question. Our case was about former players.

Second, the question of whether college athletes should be paid is a complicated topic that can't be answered yes or no. It really depends on what the questioner has in mind when asking that question. Should they be paid for their labor, or should they be paid for the use of their names, images, and likenesses? Or both? There's a lot to unpack there. And if they should be paid, *how* would they be paid? Would it be through higher dollar-value scholarships, or through wages? And *when* would they be paid—while in school, or through a trust from which they can draw after school?

This is why I would've used the word "maybe" in my interview with Kanigher. Unlike the NCAA, I'm open to discussion about how to pay college athletes. There are many ways that it could be done. The key is to ensure fairness for everyone involved and to make sure college sports continue to be so popular and beloved.

But that's not how the NCAA does business. To them, the world consists of rigid, nonnegotiable rules that are designed to protect the interests of the powerful and that must be preserved at all costs.

Sorry, NCAA. Those rules will eventually be toppled.

And they know it.

CHAPTER 4

———

TIP-OFF NEARS

FOLLOWING MY DEPOSITION, THE TRIAL DATE OF JUNE 9, 2014, was set. Michael Hausfeld and the rest of the legal team began to discuss trial strategies with me. One topic that I hadn't expected was whether a jury or Judge Wilken alone would decide the outcome.

Not being an attorney, I had assumed the trial would take place before a jury. Trials that I've followed before, like O.J. Simpson's trial, were before juries. Plus, trials are always depicted in movies and on TV shows as having juries. I figured the judge is sort of like a referee, a person who makes sure trial rules are enforced and followed, while the jury is kind of like a group of scorers sitting at the scorers' table.

And to be honest, I was looking forward to having a jury of

my peers listen to me and to NCAA officials. I wanted real, ordinary people judging amateurism as a system. I had envisioned being on the witness stand and looking over to my left and seeing men and women of all races and ages watching me from the jury box. I could see them diligently taking notes and imagined them nodding in agreement when I spoke, too, like, *We totally get what you're saying, Ed.*

I knew I could connect with jurors and explain where I was coming from, which was a genuine desire to see college basketball and college sports in general thrive. I cherish basketball beyond words.

. . .

At Avalon Gardens Elementary School in Los Angeles, California, I was a lot taller than everyone else and naturally gravitated toward hoops. I kept getting better at it. I played on traveling teams. I played in summer camps. I was always playing.

What I especially like about basketball is that there's always a benchmark to meet and a new goal that follows. One day you're able to dunk on a short rim that's just a few feet high. And then as you grow, your parents adjust the rim higher and higher. So each dunk is more satisfying than the last. Then, some years later, a day comes when you can touch the glass on a regulation rim. You think, *This is getting real.* And then one day, still further out, you're tall enough to touch the actual rim. It's a great feeling—but not as great as when you can dunk a golf ball, then a tennis ball, and then a volleyball.

The best feeling, though, occurs on a truly magical day: the day when you can dunk a basketball on a regulation rim. All of those hours of practice and all of those squat exercises finally pay off.

That sense of achievement is what made basketball so fulfilling for me and is one of the main reasons why I spent eight years in court trying to protect this sport. I could see myself getting better all the time, and learning the intricacies of the game. That's what basketball and sports should be about—getting better all the time at what you invest so much time in.

The truth is, basketball defined my childhood and played a big role in shaping the man I became. When I think back to the '80s, I remember that my friends and I would ride our Diamondback dirt bikes over to the local arcade and play *Donkey Kong* and *Pac-Man*. Sometimes we'd get a milkshake. And then we'd head over to the park and play pickup hoops.

Back then, basketball had nothing to do with business. There were no agents around us. There were no handlers looking to talk to the parents and cousins of the best players. No one from any sneaker company was writing feverishly on a notepad about every move we made.

It was just the love of the sport.

So it's not surprising that some of my most enjoyable moments in life happened while on a basketball court.

I remember the day when I first dunked on a regulation hoop. It was 1985 and I was twelve years old. At six foot two, I was the tallest person in my class at Peary Junior High in the LA neighborhood of Gardena. People would tell me I'd grow to seven feet tall like Kareem Abdul-Jabbar. I got up there, but not quite *there*.

Well, that day my buddies and I were playing basketball outside during our physical education course. It was the last class of the day, too. We weren't really playing—we were trying to dunk! And three or four of us were getting pretty close. We stuck around the court for over an hour, even after school got out. We were determined to do it.

As our classmates walked out of the school, they headed for

home or for the school bus. But then they noticed what we were doing. Like us, they became fixated on our dunk attempts. They walked over to watch the dunk contest. Except this wasn't a dunk contest where the goal was the most stylish dunk. This was a contest where the goal was *any* dunk. We attracted quite the crowd, and many of them were girls. They were all cheering us on. And, well, when you're twelve years old, there's no telling what you can do on a basketball court with girls watching! There's also a certain feeling you get when you're on center stage and people are taking the time to watch you perform. There's something special about that.

Anyway, I kept getting close to a dunk but was just slightly off. On some attempts I didn't leap high enough. At times my approach speed was too slow and at other times I dribbled too high, which hurt my arc as I jumped. On a few tries I took off from the ground too far out. No matter the cause, I wasn't above the rim.

There were also attempted dunks where I had the height but couldn't fully control the ball, so I missed getting it through the rim. Ball control is an underrated skill for a young basketball player, and one that takes a while to develop. A lot of people assume that dunking is all about a player's height and how high he or she can jump. Those are important factors, to be sure. But just like there's "an art of a deal," there's an art of a dunk. It's an art that takes a while to achieve.

Well, then finally it happened. On one drive, I truly had momentum on my side. I drove as hard as I could to the basket and picked up a lot of speed along the way. I took off in the sweet spot for a dunk, which is right before the rim but not quite under it. And I had full control of the ball as I entered the air space. As I climbed in the air, I saw the rim approach and the ball was secure in my left hand—I'm a lefty. Then I got it just over the rim for the dunk! Man, everyone went crazy. I felt like I was on cloud nine. It may not have looked like a Dominique Wilkins tomahawk jam or a Dr. J epic throwdown, but it was a dunk and it felt incredible.

The first time I dunked in an actual game was just as satisfying.

It happened during my freshman year at Verbum Dei High School in Watts, an LA neighborhood you've probably heard of from your history books. I played on the varsity team. I was one of those kids who was good enough to be on varsity, and even good enough to start, but I didn't play a whole lot. This is the way it worked: the coach thought you had potential and if you got rolling in a game, cool, you'd get minutes. But if you didn't, the coach would sub you out and you'd get garbage time at the end.

We were about to play in a preseason tournament in River Side, over an hour away from Watts. On the ride over we listened to the Beastie Boys' new tape, *Licensed to Ill*. It got me pumped, even if the dad of my teammate who was driving hated every second of it!

Our game didn't go too well, though. We were down by about thirty points with a few minutes to go. As often happens in blowouts, both teams had their scrubs in. I was one of those scrubs, at least on that day. By this point, most of the people in the stands had already left. You couldn't really blame them, either—the game wasn't competitive at all. And most of the ones still left seemed focused on their conversations and the games coming up. But I cared. See, I always played hard. *Always*. No matter the circumstances and no matter whether it made a difference in the outcome of the game.

Why?

Because it was the grind of basketball that I loved the most.

The many hours of shooting jump shots and free throws. Sometimes I'd do all that alone. Sometimes my dad and brother Charles would be standing right next to me, watching and critiquing. Then there were the many hours of practice, where you're exhausted from sprinting up and down the court but you keep going—you don't stop. And then all those times you spend in the locker room going over plays with teammates and making sure everyone has them down pat. All of it counted, no matter the score.

So there I was, playing in a blowout game in front of an audience that couldn't have cared less.

But I'm playing tight defense and not letting the kid I'm covering advance. Then I see an opportunity to poke the ball from him and steal it. I do just that.

I'm then dribbling on the right side of the floor, and the person who threw the ball away gives up chase. That's when I realize—this is it, my opportunity to dunk!

I keep driving and driving. And I keep picking up speed. I jump, and dunk the ball!

The fact that I did it, I honestly couldn't believe it. My teammates went crazy. The crowd didn't care, but I sure did.

Basketball wasn't just a sport for me. It also served as a compass on the map of life.

When I was about eleven or twelve, I'd spend countless hours playing football and basketball right around the elementary school. Immediately in front of the school was a lawn that went as wide as the school itself and right next to it was a playground with a basketball court. After school, we'd play football on the lawn and then hop the fence and play hoops.

I'd always bring Charles with me, in part because our father said I couldn't go unless I brought Charles along with me. And Dad made clear that Charles and I must always be on the same team, too. We could never be rivals. That stayed true through college, as both of us played at UCLA.

But back when Charles and I were kids, lots of our friends and other local kids played basketball in that park at the school.

Two O'Bannon boys catching the basketball bug early. Charles is little number four and I'm little number eight.

Some were a little bit older than me. Since I was tall and relatively advanced as an athlete, I'd often play with the older kids. And like any other kid, I was impressionable, especially when around kids who were a little bit older.

Not all influences are good.

You see, the Bloods recruited from this playground. It's worth emphasizing that this was the early '80s. My neighborhood was Blood territory. If you wanted to be associated with being a gang member you wore the color red. Not only your clothing but your shoes, hat, belt, and bandana as well. It wasn't uncommon for LA gangs to identify young basketball players as potential gang members. And around twelve or thirteen years old were the ages when either you began to gangbang and hang out with a certain crowd or you didn't. It was a crossroads.

The Bloods were hard to miss. They patrolled their turf like they were some kind of police force or army. They usually wore distinctive clothing, almost like uniforms, so you knew who they were—red shirts and sometimes with red hats on their heads and red bandanas in their back pockets. Many of them also wore sagging pants that often showed a little bit too much. Their arms and necks also displayed certain kinds of tattoos. They sure knew who you were, too. Like coaches would watch how you play, gangs would watch how you interact. You were always under their eye.

One day I was practicing free throws and wearing a backward baseball cap. It was my old Little League cap for the team I played for, the Cubs. Like the real Cubs, the hat had the big *C* on the front, except our hats were red instead of Chicago blue. I noticed this gangbanger walking around the playground, checking things out. He saw me and quickly hopped the fence. He got in my face and said, "Yo, what's up with the *C?* What are you trying to be, Crips?" I quickly reassured him, "No way, man. It's *C* for the Cubs Little League team. Nothing to do with anything else. Seriously." This dude wasn't fully appeased. "I suggest you take this hat off right now," he commanded. I heeded his advice and threw the hat into the thrash, with him watching every moment of it.

My life as a young basketball player wasn't immune from what was going on in Los Angeles back in the '80s and '90s. I steered clear of the trouble—but one day I got an unexpected and unwanted assist. It seemed like a typical day. Charles and I were playing hoops after school at the park. I was twelve at the time and Charles was ten. Some of the older kids said they wanted to "go kick it." Charles and I were just two kids who knew a lot about basketball, arcade games, and dirt bikes—we had no idea what the older kids were going to do. We were curious, though. We didn't have an actual invitation, but figured we'd just blend in. It was cool, we thought.

Well, one of the older kids who had joined the Bloods noticed us. He walked right in front of us, and raised his right hand and almost put it directly on my face. He said, "Yo, stop." His name was Tommy. He was a couple of years older than me. Pretty good baller but he had joined the Bloods and started down that path of life. "You need to stay back, yo!" Tommy yelled at us. "You can't come with us."

This was clearly a command and not a suggestion. And I didn't like it. "Wait, what?" I pleaded, "We just want to check it out—you won't notice us there, we just want to see what's going on." I thought I was being picked on, or, worse, that I just wasn't cool enough to go with them. "Look, man," Tommy barked back, "you're really good at ball. You have a future in this. Don't blow it over stupid stuff like this."

I kept trying to come up with a reason that would let us stick with the group, but to no avail. Tommy chuckled. "Hey, look, Ed. One day when you're playing ball in college and the NBA, I'll come and check you out. I mean it." I wasn't impressed by Tommy's compliments or his so-called promise to look me up years from then. I thought he was just coming up with excuses to exclude me. "Whatever, man," I replied.

I went home that day really upset. I thought I had screwed up or—worse still—maybe there was something wrong with me. Like I didn't make the mark or something like that. I felt like a loser.

Well, eight years later, that so-called rejection came full circle.

I was coming out of the UCLA locker room after a game. I was going to walk to my car and drive to my apartment, as I usually did. I expected the normal scene, which meant a handful of journalists and fans standing right outside the locker room door. Sometimes they'd ask questions or pay a compliment or two. This time, however, I noticed someone who didn't look like a UCLA student or a *Los Angeles Times* writer. It was a black man in his early to mid-twenties, and he was standing about twenty feet away from the locker room door.

He wasn't dressed as a Blood by any means. He was wearing regular jeans and a polo shirt. He seemed like a guy you'd see walking in a shopping mall or a department store. At the same time, he was a little bit older than a college student and, unlike a lot of journalists, he was comfortably standing from a distance and not making any moves to try to talk to me. He was also making eye contact with me as I walked in his direction. I couldn't quite place it, but I knew the face.

It hit me who he was as he spoke first. "Yo, Ed."

"Tommy?"

He smiled. "I came to check on you, man, just like I said I would. Dude, you can play!"

I couldn't believe it. I gave him a big hug. We spoke for only a couple of minutes, but he told me he had turned his life around and was no longer in a gang. He had a job and was doing fine. I thanked him for coming out. The thing is, I wasn't really thanking him for watching me play or for saying nice things about my game. I was thanking him for setting me straight as a kid.

That was the last time I ever saw Tommy. Wherever he is, Tommy held all the power in the world over that twelve-year-old kid I once was. And it was because of his decency as a human

Together my brother and I steered clear of the gang lifestyle that was all too prevalent in the Los Angeles of our youth.

and my abilities as a basketball player that I kept walking down the right path.

You can be sure that when I fight for basketball, whether it's the hardwood court or in a court of law, I'm fighting for a game that can change a life.

* * *

But I never got to share those basketball life stories with jurors, because I never encountered them. As I learned, juries aren't automatic in trials. With the parties' consent, the judge can act as the jury. And in some cases it makes sense to go in that direction.

A few months before the trial, Michael called and told me the legal team was at a crossroads. They wanted to hear what I thought about whether we should use a jury or go with Judge Wilken. Michael prefaced his question by saying that they had conducted a mock trial before a group of people who had agreed to act as jurors.

It didn't go well—at all.

For one, the group found our antitrust arguments to be complicated and confusing. Antitrust law doesn't exactly roll off the tongue. It focuses not on what is "right" in a moral sense but on what maximizes competition in a given market. To determine how competition is maximized, both sides offer opposing views about how to judge competitiveness and define the relevant market. For example, the NCAA and our side argued over whether Division I college sports is a recognizable market for purposes of antitrust law.

Because of this focus on competition, we weren't assured of victory even if we proved what, to me, seemed like the crucial point: that college athletes and former college athletes should be paid more than nothing for the use of their names, images, and likenesses. Instead, we'd win only if we showed that the NCAA and its members acted as a cartel that fixed prices in ways that courts have recognized to be anticompetitive under the Sherman Act. Getting there would require educating jurors about economic theories and asking them to endorse legal arguments about the NCAA that hadn't before been considered by courts. Based on feedback from the focus group, a jury might not see the law our way.

The other problem, Michael explained, was that the focus group dwelled on college athletes already receiving full scholarships. Some in the focus group took that to mean college athletes must already be doing okay. It's the same perspective referenced several times in this book: a lot of people believe that athletes who receive a free ride to college have no legitimate grievance about their state of affairs.

Several others in the focus group saw it more along our line of thinking—to a point, at least. They believed that college athletes have a legitimate stake in the commercial use of their identities. But they didn't take the next logical step. They voiced a belief that while college athletes have the stronger moral argument, the law doesn't necessarily compel the NCAA to act.

When Michael filled me in on those details, I thought of what my parents would often ask Charles and me while we were growing up: "You might want something, but do you need it?" As our preachers told us, God gives you what you need, not what you want. If jurors saw our arguments that way, we'd be in a lot of trouble.

So when Michael mentioned that we could petition Judge Wilken to decide the case, I told him that sounded like the way to go. I asked him, though, if he had a sense of where Judge Wilken stood in terms of the arguments. Was she on our side? Michael sounded confident but cautious. "Ed," Michael replied in his trademark carefully worded way, "we believe we have a great legal argument—and not just a moral or ethical argument—that the NCAA has illegally set to $0 the value of your name, image, and likeness. It can't do that, especially when it sells those video games and TV rights with you in them for billions of dollars. At the end of the day, their argument doesn't make any sense—if the value was really $0, then they wouldn't have made all this money. They can't have it both ways. So we not only have the better moral argument, we have the better legal argument, too. You can never really predict what a judge will do, but I believe Judge Wilken will agree."

We were thus set for a trial before Judge Wilken, and she would pick the winner.

We then talked about our witness list and the order of witnesses. Michael asked me if I felt comfortable going first. I responded, "Hell, yes. That's exactly what I want." I truly loved the idea of being the first witness. I'd be able to share my story and set the tone from day one. I also liked the idea of going first and getting it over with.

The fact that I had already testified in the deposition made me feel confident, too. At least to some degree, I knew what to expect while on the witness stand. I knew the NCAA would try to get me flustered and attempt to make me sound angry and confused. *Don't let them.* I knew I should only answer the specific question asked and not let my answer go beyond it. And I knew to pause before answering a question from the NCAA, because one of our lawyers might object to the question.

The trial was expected to go about three weeks. Rosa and I arrived in town a couple of days before, just to settle in. When we hopped into a cab I texted Pam Vaccaro, *We're here. Game time!* Pam responded that she and Mr. Vaccaro were excited too. This was finally happening.

Rosa and I obviously took the trip seriously, but we also promised ourselves that we were going to give ourselves some down time. We went out to dinner in Oakland and went to watch the A's at the Coliseum. During our time in the city we saw the A's play the Red Sox and I got to watch David Ortiz bat, which was awesome.

It seemed everywhere we went had a connection to the case in some form or another. This was even true of our hotel, the downtown Marriott. It was attached to the building where the Golden State Warriors practice. Bob Myers, the team's general manager, and I had played together at UCLA. He knew exactly what I was fighting for.

On the day before the trial, June 8, we visited Michael's office in San Francisco and met up with the rest of the legal team. We then did a mock trial and Michael questioned me as if he were the NCAA. At one point he thought my answer went on too long. "Answer the specific questions," Michael barked at me, "and then shut the hell up." He also gave me fairly direct suggestions about demeanor, body language, and posture. "Ed, keep your head up and don't blow up." The mock trial got pretty intense at times—we were dead serious about what we were doing.

CHAPTER 5

GAME TIME

ROSA AND I AWOKE EARLY ON JUNE 9 AT THE MARRIOTT, A COUPLE of blocks from the courthouse. Rosa ordered room service and we were both getting into game mode. I reviewed my notes and worked on my voice to make sure I sounded okay. I was going to be the leadoff hitter and I wanted to make it count.

As we walked over to the courthouse, my phone rang. It was Harry Flournoy, who had joined the case back in 2010 and phoned me regularly. He was a hero of mine and was a source of sanity—he knew how to put things in perspective. That morning he told me, "Ed, don't forget what this is all about: human rights. It's not right to make money off the backs of others and deny them pay. You're standing up for justice, young man, and we're all grateful for it."

I felt inspired and ready to go.

When we arrived at the courthouse there was a long line of people outside the door to go through security. There were lawyers everywhere. There must have been fifty of them. It was unbelievable. I spotted Pam and Mr. Vaccaro in the line. He gave me a big thumbs-up and I smiled. We were almost there.

When Rosa and I entered the courtroom I sat at the plaintiff's table. My emotions were intact and I had my water ready. Judge Wilken then walked in and introductions were made. Within a few minutes, boom, I'm on the stand! It happened so fast.

It was around 8:45 a.m. when I was sworn in. I would be on the stand for about two and a half hours.

The moment I took the stand I thought back to the day we started this whole thing, Tuesday, July 21, 2009.

• • •

When I got to work that day I decided to let a few people in on a big secret: I was about to sue the NCAA.

I first told Rick Glenn, which I thought was fitting because he was the guy who had taken me to Mike Curtis's house to see Spencer play me in the video game. That day I also told our general manager, Rich Abajian, as well as my brother, Charles. Two of those three guys looked at me as if I were from Mars.

Charles and Rick just couldn't believe it. "How does anyone file a lawsuit against the NCAA?" Rick joked in disbelief. "Nobody does that!"

Word in the dealership spread fast. I remember being in the showroom and salespeople kept coming up to me and saying, "Ed, what are you doing? You're fighting city hall, man!" One by one, it happened all day.

Once the lawsuit was filed, the interview requests came in like an avalanche. My phone wouldn't stop ringing, and all these random texts came in. I don't know how everyone suddenly had my phone number. Did someone post somewhere, *Here's Ed O'Bannon's phone number?*

I'll be honest. I said to myself, *Holy shit, what did I get myself into here? What am I really doing?* I knew sports fans would be interested in the case, but this went way beyond that. I had news reporters and TV producers calling me nonstop. I went online and saw article after article about the lawsuit, and some of the readers' comments weren't too flattering.

Then the emails poured in. I couldn't do my work.

For a little bit of time that day, I kind of regretted the case. You see, I had gotten used to a routine—I'd show up at work, work hard, drive home, see my wife and family, and talk. This lawsuit looked like it might disrupt that. I kind of knew that would happen and both Mr. Vaccaro and Jon had warned me. But when it actually happened, it felt different—much worse than I had anticipated.

But as the hours went by, I realized that the first day would be different from the others. This was a big news story today but would be less so tomorrow and even less the day after that. Sure, the case would generate headlines from time to time, but on most days I went about my normal routine.

• • •

So, I knew on the stand that it might be strange at first but I'd become more familiar with it as it went along. And, in truth, those two and a half hours on the stand consisted of some of the most fun I had experienced in a long time. I absolutely loved being up there. I couldn't believe how calm I felt. It's weird for me to say that, but it's true.

There were a couple of reasons why.

First, this was our moment—our chance to stand up to the NCAA and face them. The fact that we had the NCAA in court was already a victory for a lot of people. I was on the stand not just for Ed O'Bannon. I was there for the thousands of athletes who, like me, the NCAA had stolen from. This was what we were fighting for. This was our chance to speak. And it was happening. And I loved every minute of it.

Second, I felt at peace because of who I saw when I looked out to the gallery. Sure, there were a lot of lawyers and media types. I saw them, scribbling and typing away. But that's not who I looked *at*. When I needed to look away, I'd look at three people, who not coincidentally sat right next to each other. Rosa, Mrs. Vaccaro, and Mr. Vaccaro.

Rosa was my strength that day, just like she is every day. She's my best friend. She's my bridge. She gives me my backbone. She is such a remarkable woman. I would just look at her and I knew everything would be okay. As a passionate and talented educator, Rosa also understood the fight and believed in it. Rosa wasn't an athlete and, despite her husband's career, has never been a sports fan. She didn't need to be into sports to understand my case.

With Rosa at my graduation in December 2011 in front of the building where we met in November 1991.

This fight is way more about justice and honesty than it is about athletics and games.

And as I sat on the witness stand and saw Rosa's beautiful eyes, I recalled her telling me about when she realized the truth about how the NCAA treats college education.

• • •

Rosa had been a guidance counselor to a female high school basketball player. This player had met with Rosa several times to discuss her college and career choices. Her strengths and interests were in math, science, and in helping people with health problems. With those factors in mind, Rosa suggested to her advisee that she consider enrolling at UNLV, which had offered her an athletic scholarship and has a really good nursing program. This young woman took Rosa's advice and accepted the athletic scholarship to attend UNLV, determined to major in nursing.

That never happened.

When Rosa's advisee met with college academic advisors, those advisors generally discouraged her from pursuing the UNLV nursing program. One advisor told her the program "would likely be too time consuming given her basketball commitments." Rosa's advisee was also warned that many majors are too difficult for someone who, like her, needs to be focused on basketball. The advisee was instead directed to study kinesiology, which, with due respect, obviously doesn't offer the same kind of career path as does a nursing program. Hospitals and clinics hire nurses right out of college. I'm sure there are career options for kinesiology majors, but many of those students are probably looking at grad school, which can be mighty costly, to advance their career.

Rosa was really upset to hear about what happened. Her

advisee was African American and the first person in her family to go to college. And just like 99 percent of college basketball players, she was never going to play professional basketball. Her college studies would shape her life and career.

This experience, along with others, led Rosa to seriously doubt the so-called free education of college athletes. Many majors for them are not options. They can't study science because it's "too hard." They can't pursue accounting because it's "too demanding." They can't major in teaching since it requires internships over the summer. They can't study abroad or take part in many other university programs available, since doing so would conflict with sports. The NCAA not only allows this framework but, through amateurism, encourages it.

* * *

When I looked at Rosa from the stand, I looked into someone who not only understood the cause but who also embraced it. This inspired me to make her proud. I then looked at the Vaccaros. They were the heart of this case, the heart of correcting an injustice. They could have enjoyed their retirement in Santa Monica and lived the good life. Instead, they chose to fight. I may have been the only one on the witness stand, but in a way Rosa, the Vaccaros, and college athletes everywhere were up there too.

Michael conducted the first part of the questioning—the "direct." I knew the kinds of questions he was going to ask because we had discussed them during our mock trial. Those questions focused on how sports came before school while I was a student at UCLA. I detailed how I was encouraged to take relatively easy courses so that I could maximize my development as a basketball player. "Don't take classes that are too hard or that will pull you out of practice," I was often told back then. The truth is, I was an athlete masquerading as a college student. I basically did the minimum to make sure I kept my academic eligibility so I could continue to play. And I told the court as much.

Now, these remarks were obviously not about video games and television rebroadcasts and how I appeared in them without consent or compensation. But they were nonetheless relevant to our case because one of the NCAA's main defenses was that compensation for college athletes would corrupt those athletes' academic experience. My testimony showed that the academic experience for top Division I college athletes was already a sham.

After Michael finished asking me questions, Glenn Pomerantz, the NCAA's lead counsel, got up from the defendant's table and began cross-examination.

I knew I was in for a battle.

I didn't like him, first and foremost. But that's not a dig. Pomerantz did his job very well in making me not like him, so in a way I say that as a compliment. And like the other NCAA attorneys, he was polite and had an air of superiority. He seemed to talk down to me and he didn't appear too concerned about what I might say. It reminded me of my basketball days when we played teams that we weren't supposed to beat. Sometimes they didn't warm up as hard and kind of looked at us like we were a joke. It's that same feeling you get when the person you're speaking with views you as beneath them. It is an unsettling feeling, and I felt it while Pomerantz spoke to me.

Pomerantz was also slick. He tried to make me sound hypocritical based on the deposition I had given in 2011. As I mentioned earlier in this book, I gave a vague response to a vague question about whether college athletes should be paid while in school, and that was before our case expanded to include current college athletes. And all that entire exchange stemmed from remarks I'm quoted as saying in a *Las Vegas Sun* article published in 2010.

Pomerantz clearly thought he had me. He did not. I told him college athletes should be paid given the amount of money they generate for schools. It's not a hard concept.

The one question that caught me off guard was his last.

After grilling me for over an hour, Pomerantz paused as if he had this momentous point. "Mr. O'Bannon," Pomerantz inquired, "should high school athletes be paid if their games are on television?" I responded yes, so long as those broadcasts are generating revenue for their schools. Then, in a self-righteous tone, Pomerantz asked, "What about Little League players appearing on TV?" I thought about it and said, "Yes, so long as they are generating revenue."

Pomerantz smirked at me like I had said something stupid. Even the people in the gallery shuffled with an uneasy sigh. I wasn't deterred, though. I continued in my testimony by saying that twelve-year-old actors get paid when they appear on television and generate revenue. It's not about being too young to get paid. Still, I could almost feel the whole courtroom look at me. I could see everyone's faces. If those faces could talk during the middle of a witness's testimony, they'd be saying, *Dude, did you seriously just say that Little Leaguers should get paid?*

I wish I could have a do-over on that answer, but not because I'd change the thrust of my answer. Yes, Little Leaguers should be paid. But I would want to explain my answer more fully. "Pay" to Little Leaguers doesn't necessarily mean a paycheck. It could mean reimbursement to the parents for travel costs, hotel room bills, and car mileage. It could mean better uniforms and equipment for the kids and improved and safer fields where they play. "Pay" could come in many forms so long as it gives back to the players' communities.

I would have also mentioned that Pomerantz's comparing the NCAA to Little League was misleading, at best. The NCAA is a cartel of more than 1,200 members that agree to rules that prevent athletes—the vast majority of whom are eighteen or older—from receiving compensation. Little League Baseball is just one company that sets rules for kids aged four to sixteen. They are structurally different and have different goals.

By the way, what happened two months after my trial? Mo'ne Davis dominated the Little League World Series and became a national sensation. She was the first girl to pitch a shutout in the history of the Little League World Series. She was on ESPN throwing heat. Everybody loved her—she's talented and charismatic. *Sports Illustrated* put her on its cover.

Davis also signed an endorsement deal with Chevrolet, even though she was only thirteen years old and wouldn't be driving for a few years. As part of that deal, she appeared in a Spike Lee–directed spot where she's shown excelling at different sports—including swishing a half-court shot on a basketball court—and while pitching she declares, "I throw seventy miles per hour. That's throwing like a girl!" Then the ad shows the text, *Chevrolet celebrates Mo'ne Davis and those who remind us that anything is possible.*

I said to myself, *Here is a Little Leaguer who signs an endorsement deal with a car company.* And I got courtroom grief for wanting Little Leaguers' parents to get gas money!

And what about the NCAA's position on Davis? Mark Emmert told media that she could take endorsement money related to baseball because baseball likely wouldn't be the sport she'd play in college. He compared Davis to Danny Ainge, who in the early '80s maintained his eligibility to play college basketball while pursuing a professional baseball career with the Toronto Blue Jays.

I'm glad the NCAA didn't try to stop Davis from endorsement deals. But why does it stop those deals with any athletes? What is the point? It's obvious that young athletes can be extremely marketable. Why not let them be?

Judge Wilken dismissed me from the witness stand. Rosa

was completely on my mind as I began to get up and walk back, just like she was on my mind for 90 percent of the testimony. Another 5 percent was on my kids and the remaining 5 percent was on trying to get back to my seat without passing out. That would have been embarrassing!

I felt genuinely relieved getting into my seat at our side's table, and was determined to show a poker face and just sit there. But my mind was on my performance. How did I do? Was I good or bad? Did anything I say make a difference? All I could do was sit and watch on.

That first break came when Judge Wilken called for the lunch recess. I didn't get to speak with Rosa first. Instead, Michael first came over to me and kindly said, "You were great, Ed. You spoke clearly and decisively. And you were authentic up there—at the end of the day, that's what matters most." Sathya, who was immediately behind Michael, then reached over and put his right hand on my shoulder. He smiled. "You nailed it, Ed."

Only after we walked away from the plaintiff's table and toward the rows where the public was seated did I get to talk to Rosa and the Vaccaros. They whispered kind things in my ear. I felt pumped, like I had just scored twenty points and pulled down a dozen rebounds.

That night Rosa and I had dinner in the Marriott's Iron and Oak Restaurant. There was a TV and ESPN was on it. At the bottom of the broadcast was a ticker where my trial was mentioned on a loop. I took it in for a moment. *This trial has really started.* We really had the NCAA in the hot seat. Man, did it feel good.

Now, I knew tweets were being sent and articles were being written about my testimony. I could have easily gone online and read the coverage.

But I didn't.

I wasn't going to get caught up in it. I had said my piece and that was all.

CHAPTER 6

THE TWO FACES OF COLLEGE SPORTS

I was glad to have my part of the trial over with, but I wasn't exactly sure how I should approach the rest of the trial. Should I show up in court the next day? If so, where should I sit? These might sound like silly questions, but it was all new to me. I had never been in a trial, not even as a juror.

I asked Michael for advice. "Ed, you're free to do what you like," he explained. "You've done your part and more—but the trial has your name on it. We would love it if you continued to attend the hearings and sat at our table."

That was all I needed to hear. I would attend the rest of the trial, take notes, and offer suggestions. Sure, I wasn't going to supply any legal advice or courtroom strategies. But I could share my expertise about college sports and how the NCAA really operates. I could also fact-check what came out of the mouths of NCAA officials. Let's just say there was a lot of hot air and "fake news."

The person I most wanted to see on the stand was NCAA President Mark Emmert. To my eyes, Emmert typifies everything wrong in college sports. I came to this conclusion back in 2011, when PBS's *Frontline* show did an episode on my case. "Money and March Madness" brought awareness of the lawsuit to a broader audience, including those who cared little about sports but a great deal about education and justice.

As part of the episode, Lowell Bergman, a professor of investigative journalism at Berkeley, interviewed Emmert. Bergman confronted Emmert with the many ways people—including Emmert himself—become rich from college sports, yet how college athletes are placed in an altogether different category. Bergman used research from sports economist Andrew Zimbalist to make this point.

Take a look at this portion of a lengthy transcript:

ANDREW ZIMBALIST: So in that system, the coach ends up getting paid the money that would otherwise go to the player. And so you have these coaches all over the map who are getting paid $2 million, $3 million, $4 million, $5 million.

LOWELL BERGMAN: Like coach John Calipari, who makes $4 million a year at Kentucky, and coach Bill Self, who makes $3 million a year at Kansas.

When Mark Emmert was president of the University of Washington and other schools, he regularly supported paying coaches in excess of a million dollars a year.

[on camera] How do you respond to economists who say that if you had to pay the market value of some of the players, particularly the star players on your teams, then you couldn't afford to pay the coaches that much?

MARK EMMERT: Well, it's an interesting but irrelevant argument. You know, the fact of the matter is, if you paid the custodians in the stands a lot more, there'd be less revenue to pay the coach. You know, what—what basis would one make that argument? The fact is, they're not employees. They're student athletes.

LOWELL BERGMAN: You don't see the contradiction that many have pointed out that when we're watching March Madness, you may have a coach who's being paid six figures, maybe seven figures in some cases—everyone is being paid—the athletic director—but the students aren't. The athletes who are actually performing are not paid.

MARK EMMERT: No, I don't find that contradictory at all. Quite the contrary. I think what would be utterly unacceptable is, in fact, to convert students into employees.

Some people say my case was about video games. That exchange with Emmert shows how it was really about taking on a flawed mindset that openly endorses athlete exploitation. It's the kind of mindset that equates custodians being paid more with athletes simply getting paid something. It's crazy. Emmert sees no problem with money being made off the athletes so others get paid. Why? Because it would "convert students into employees."

First off, that's not necessarily true. Whether a person is an "employee" is a fairly complicated legal topic that's well beyond my understanding of the law. But suffice it to say, it's not as simple as Emmert contends. Second, and more importantly, we weren't asking for athletes to get paid for their labor, as do custodians who maintain the cleanliness of an arena. We were asking if athletes had the right to negotiate for the commercial use of their names, images, and likenesses. That's all.

Now, I don't usually remember my dreams. I know some people do, but for me, I wake up and it's about whether I feel rested. But the night following my testimony I slept better than

I had in months. I was so exhausted from the experience that I passed out on our hotel bed. I entered a kind of deep sleep that I've been in only a few times in my life.

And I had dreams that I would recall the next morning.

I dreamed of Judge Wilken's courtroom, with NCAA officials taking the stand, one after the next.

I dreamed of these pompous-looking guys, dressed to the nines, sitting anxiously. I couldn't quite make out their faces, but I could see them squirm and fidget while trying to defend the indefensible. I could see them flustered and angered while talking to my lawyers who didn't fall for their verbal head-fakes. And I could see Judge Wilken sitting nearby, puzzled not only by what these officials were saying but by how arrogantly they said it. *Finally*, I thought, *someone is judging them!*

And they would have to face me. *The whole damn time.*

Even better, they'd have to face the tens of thousands of young people that my case represented.

When the actual trial brought NCAA officials to the stand, I made sure to make eye contact with each and every one of them. This was especially true when Emmert took the stand on June 19, 2014. I looked right into his eyes as he stumbled to answer question after question. I almost felt bad for him.

Almost.

Emmert had to justify "amateurism," the NCAA principle that college athletes can't be paid for their labor or for the commercial use of their names, images, and likenesses because such pay would be…exploitative.

That's right. To the NCAA, paying athletes is exploitation while denying them pay is protection. Only in the NCAA's upside-down world does that make any sense.

My lawyer, Bill Isaacson, showed Emmert picture after picture of college athletes hawking different companies. There were University of Iowa football players wearing Nike uniforms and a poster of those players with the Nike "swoosh" shown above their heads. There was a national championship program with former college stars placed next to various corporate sponsors. There was a trading card of star Florida State University quarterback Jameis Winston selling for $29.95.

It went on and on.

None of those athletes received a dime for endorsing products they had no choice but to endorse. In fact, if they had been paid, they'd have been thrown off their teams like trespassers, forfeited their athletic scholarships, and become pariahs on campus. They might not have been able to afford to stick around.

But someone got paid for those player endorsements. The NCAA and its member institutions—which include nearly 1,300 colleges and conferences—take in billions of dollars from licensing athletes' images.

At one point Bill asked Emmert, "Putting athletes in front of logos, that's all fine under NCAA rules?" Emmert smugly replied, "It's fine under the rules."

The rules.

NCAA executives say their rules protect "tradition" and encourage "cohesion." They fear what college campuses might look like if college athletes were compensated, in one form or another, for their labor and likenesses. If paid, the NCAA says, college athletes would view themselves as different from their classmates. And the rest of the campus would see them as different, too.

As if that isn't already the case!

Look, for decades college athletes have lived lives that are totally unlike their classmates'. It is dishonest to pretend otherwise. I know this all too well because I experienced it at UCLA back in the '90s.

I spent more than fifty hours per week playing games, traveling, working out, practicing, attending meetings, and doing about a dozen other things for my teams. At the same time, I was expected to juggle a full-time class schedule that only permitted courses at times that didn't interfere with sports. And I had to be around campus over the summer, too.

And let's look at nonathlete students. At a lot of schools, they aren't allowed to work more than fifteen or twenty hours a week. Why? Because their education comes first. And unless you're an athlete, course selection is treated as an academic matter—not a "don't interfere with football practice or basketball practice" issue. And in a nonathlete student's spare time and over the summer, he or she can do whatever they want. Their freedom might have something to do with the fact that, unlike college athletes, they're not generating billions of dollars in revenue.

Don't get me wrong: the life of a college athlete has a lot of perks. But to claim it is just like the life of other college students is total fantasy.

The rules aren't about protection or about preserving an imaginary old-world order. They're about commercially exploiting teenagers and young adults, many of whom are, like me, black.

Yep, I said black. Let's be honest here. The vast majority of NCAA revenue is generated through the March Madness tournament, which features basketball teams made up of mostly black players. And even though the NCAA itself doesn't directly profit from college football since football revenue flows to conferences and colleges, a majority of Division I Football Bowl Subdivision college football players are black too.

Let me put it this way: The athletes whose labor and likenesses generate the vast majority of money from college sports are mostly black. And colleges knowingly adopt rules to not pay those athletes. Don't you think there's something wrong here?

Now, I'm not arguing that the NCAA is deliberately racist. I don't think they're sitting around a table, looking at each other with evil grins, saying, "Let's make billions of dollars off of black kids and let's make sure they aren't paid any of it!" But sometimes racism comes from rules that claim to treat everyone equally. You know, so-called neutral rules.

Take a rule that treats all college athletes the same: no college athlete gets paid anything. It sounds fair, right? Every college athlete, no matter race, gender, or sport, gets treated the same. But is that rule fair when it disproportionately hurts black college athletes? And is it fair when no college athlete had a seat at the table when that rule was being discussed and debated?

This isn't just an issue with college sports. The same could be said about eligibility rules for pro sports. There are only three major US professional sports leagues that require a player to wait until at least a year after high school before becoming eligible. As luck would have it, those are also the only three majority-black leagues: the NBA, WNBA, and NFL. All of the other major US professional sports leagues—Major League Baseball, the NHL, golf, tennis, skiing, snowboarding, you name it—let you in right after high school or even long before. And they're all majority-white leagues.

It's really hard to believe that this is all a mere coincidence that has nothing to do with race.

Court proceedings on the day after Emmert testified were also memorable. Rosa and I made our way to the courthouse that Friday morning and stood in a crowded corridor next to Judge Claudia Wilken's Oakland courtroom.

I made eye contact with an older guy standing about fifteen feet from us. He looked familiar and seemed to be making some kind of attempt to grab my attention. That in and of itself wasn't all that strange. I'm a six-foot-eight black guy. I usually tower over everyone around me. People tend to look at me because I look different from everyone else in a room. And people pretty much automatically assume I must have played in the NBA.

I was also, you know, the guy suing the NCAA—the guy,

my critics irrationally feared, who was threatening to end college sports.

We exchanged pleasantries, and I realized he was Jim Delany, the Big Ten Conference commissioner. Later that morning Delany would testify about how college athletes shouldn't be paid anything. And he'd defend an NCAA system that I believe openly exploits college football and basketball players. But while talking with me one-on-one, Delany was friendly.

I shook his hand, but man, the things I wish I had told him.

The NCAA guys never thought this day would come. For years they tried to dismiss my lawsuit, filing motion after motion, brief after brief.

They had reason to feel confident. In the past, they'd always been able to get lawsuits tossed from court for one reason or another. Some of those cases were dismissed, others settled. None, though, ever threatened their system.

Until now.

I don't think they realized that I didn't sue to negotiate a settlement. I sued to win, even knowing that whether we won or lost, I wouldn't get paid a penny.

I've never been paid from this case and I never will be paid. But I absolutely love college sports and I'm really worried about its future. Furthermore, I want justice. Those who have been in power over college sports have created rules that are fundamentally unfair to players. The way things are just won't last. The system will collapse unless we do something about it. So I brought a case not just for players—I brought it for sports itself.

And when I say "players," I'm not talking about LeBron James or Michael Jordan, nor am I referring to Tom Brady or Mike Trout. Players in the major professional sports leagues do just fine. I know that from personal experience. I was a lottery pick in the 1995 NBA draft and played in the NBA for a couple of seasons. The lives of players in the NBA, NFL, MLB, and

NHL are not my concern. I'm talking about the young people who play college sports. And I'm talking about the middle-aged men and women, husbands and wives, and fathers and mothers those young athletes will later become. Relatively few of them will ever play in a pro game. But every one of them will play their heart out for their school. And many students, alumni, and fans will closely watch them—and buy associated merchandise and apparel—along the way.

Take the typical college basketball player at a Division I men's program. He'll be commercialized all the time while in college. He'll be shown on TV wearing his uniform. His image will be streamed continuously over the internet and stored in digital files. If he's a star, a replica of his jersey will be sold.

That commercialization will continue long after his last day on campus, too. When he's in his thirties or forties or even fifties he might unexpectedly appear in an NCAA advertisement or TV commercial. Or maybe he'll see his likeness on a trading card or campus brochure. He might even hear his name called by Dick Vitale in a college basketball video game. You never quite know.

But what you *do* know is that this system makes money—a lot of money. College sports generate billions of dollars a year. And every year more money is made than in the previous year. The NCAA, colleges, commissioners, athletic directors, coaches, and other institutional players all share in the fruits of this system.

The *actual* players don't share, though. Not while they're in school. Not long afterward. Never.

But don't they get free rides in college? Yes, many of them do. And at some schools, reimbursement for tuition, books, and housing is worth around $70,000 a year. Like I mentioned earlier, that's a heck of a lot of money. Trust me, I know. Again, I'm a father with children in college. I'm well aware of how expensive college has become.

But "a free ride" doesn't make the system right or fair. It

doesn't mean that the players, some of whom are from poverty, can afford a normal college life, like being able to pay for new clothes, cell phone services, and plane tickets to go home. Nor does it mean that the players who suffer injuries—whether those injuries heal while in college or remain for a lifetime—receive adequate and lasting healthcare. And it sure doesn't mean that the players, including the many who care deeply about learning—you know, the whole point of college!—obtain a legitimate college education. A so-called "free college education" doesn't guarantee any of those things.

It also doesn't justify a peculiar set of rules that can be found nowhere else in America. Does a free college education explain why players lose their NCAA eligibility if they are paid by someone who has nothing to do with their education and who merely wants to license their identities? And does a free education justify why nothing can be paid to former players, even decades after their last college class, when businesses commercialize their collegiate identities?

All of this breeds resentment. And the resentment isn't just about counting dollars. It's about basic dignity. It's about respect. It's about treating other people fairly and ethically.

Some believe that the way things are in college sports are etched in stone and can't change. They're wrong. College sports can be made better and fairer for all.

For instance, I don't advocate college football players and basketball players getting paid millions of dollars or breaking the bank. In fact, they shouldn't get a dime more from their school than any other student athlete, male or female, in their program. Indeed, spread the money equally throughout the athletic department.

That's right.

Any increased compensation from a school to its athletes, whether we're talking about the star quarterback on the football team or the second-string setter on the women's volleyball team, should be equal. Make it fair. Make it simple. Make it focused on helping college athletes be able to live normal lives as college students. It's not that hard.

Mr. Delany earns more than $3 million a year in salary as commissioner of the Big Ten. An impressive amount, to be sure. But it gets better. Since the Big Ten has been rolling in TV dollars in recent years, Delany in 2017 earned an additional $20 million in bonus payments.

Twenty million dollars. For a guy who doesn't play. For a guy who, a few months before my trial, disingenuously warned journalists that my case threatened to make college sports unprofitable for schools. He actually claimed that if I won, the Big Ten would be forced to abandon Division I athletics and join Division III, where there are no athletic scholarships. So what actually happened after I won? The Big Ten not only didn't walk away from big-time athletics but brought in more revenue from sports than ever before.

It's mind-boggling when some people claim that compensating college athletes would break the system.

Now, I don't resent Delany getting paid all of that money. Kudos to him and whoever negotiated his employment contract. This is a free country and I'm glad it is. But what did he do to earn tens of millions of dollars when the athletes whose labor generated "his" success don't get any of it?

It doesn't take a philosophy professor to know that this system is wrong, and it doesn't take a math professor to fix it.

My ideas aren't just about moving money around. It's much more important that the NCAA and colleges empower college athletes with a *real voice* and *real say*. Under current NCAA rules, decision making about athletes is left to various administrators and school officials. Is it any surprise that the NCAA adopts rules that view athletes as indentured servants when those same athletes are cut out of the rulemaking process?

That must change. The more the NCAA and colleges view college athletes as partners, the better college sports will become.

The fact is, college sports HAVE TO change. The system is under attack from all sides.

Some lawsuits, like mine, demand that players' intellectual property rights be recognized and rewarded. Other lawsuits, like Title IX cases against Baylor University, demand that colleges take their educational—and ethical—missions seriously.

Consumers are also changing, especially young ones who are ditching cable TV for Hulu and picking Twitter over *SportsCenter* to watch game highlights. They're creating a new world for sports entertainment in the process. Competition over viewers' attention keeps leading to new innovations, too. It's a beautiful thing.

For its part, the NCAA is vulnerable to losing its lofty perch over college sports. Conferences, some of which have their own TV networks, are increasingly realizing that they don't need the NCAA anymore. And smart people are imagining ways to entice schools to leave the NCAA. People are really starting to think outside the box now. And if there's one thing the NCAA doesn't like, it's that.

The NCAA is also threatened from developments abroad. Countries like China and Israel are investing in professional sports leagues that are competing more and more with the NCAA for American players. Players no longer automatically assume that college is the place to play, right out of high school. Everything is up for grabs right now. Nothing can be taken for granted. This is a truly transformative era.

CHAPTER 7

THE REAL JURORS

I REMEMBER TALKING TO MOM AND DAD AFTER I TESTIFIED. They told me how proud they were that I was taking a stand for something I believed in and pursuing it all the way to a federal courthouse. Deep down, though, I kind of sensed that my parents had reservations about the whole thing. They knew I wasn't going to get paid anything from this case, which I think they found to be admirable but also a little bit strange.

And they knew that I had become a villain to a lot of people. I suspect that if my parents took a truth serum, they would admit that they wished I wasn't the guy doing this. I bet it was hard for them to sit back and watch this lawsuit play out.

And that makes sense. At least to some degree, this case changed my public reputation from former college basketball star to "that guy who sued the NCAA over video games." I'm not sure my folks were ready for that, or for the backlash I faced. I know they were proud of me, and I have no doubt they admired that their son was fighting to help others rather than himself. But I'm certain it was hard on them, too. When you do something like this you don't always realize all of the consequences. I wish I could have taken all of the negatives and kept them to myself.

But that wasn't realistic.

The people around me felt the pressures of this lawsuit just like I had. And I was going to have to accept that as part of the price for justice.

My parents also recognized that I sued the NCAA at a time in my life when I really didn't need to. And, yes, I sued the NCAA even though I knew that I wouldn't be paid if I won. The lawsuit was all about changing the rules. People mistakenly thought—and some, including certain ESPN broadcasters, still mistakenly think—that I sued as part of a money grab. They said, "He must be broke," and, "He must have blown all of that money he made playing hoops."

Nah. We were living just fine and the lawsuit wasn't about my getting paid anything. It was about changing a corrupt system and making college sports better. If anything, to be honest, I'd lose money if you factor in the value of time and energy. Had my critics bothered to learn more about the lawsuit, they'd have learned what my case was actually about. But I guess it's easier to attack first and learn later—if you ever bother to learn.

So why would I disrupt my life and the lives of my wife and children just to sue the NCAA and its cadre of lawyers? Why would I agree to become a threat to the dozens of influential journalists and the many millions of rabid college sports fans who—more than anything else—feared change? And why do it without the upside of any financial reward?

The truth is, for nearly twenty years, I had longed to take on the NCAA and stop its injustices. These feelings came long before

I saw a video game avatar of me doing a jump hook with my left hand, all net. I wanted to use whatever resources I had—whether it was educating others or, years later, bringing my arguments to court—to make college sports better and fairer. In a lot of ways, I was just waiting for the right moment. And I honestly didn't care about not making money. This was about preventing others from experiencing the unfairness that my teammates, my rivals, and I all experienced. That's worth way more than any monetary reward.

• • •

My issues with the NCAA trace back to 1990, when I was a senior at Artesia High School in Lakewood, California.

Even though I was a California kid through and through, my heart was set on playing at the University of Nevada at Las Vegas. The Runnin' Rebels had just won the national championship by beating the so-called invincible Duke Blue Devils by thirty points. UNLV had it all. They had college basketball's best coach and best assistant coach with Jerry Tarkanian and Tim Grgurich. And they had Stacey Augmon, Anderson Hunt, and of course Larry Johnson, who was the greatest player in the world to me. I wanted to play alongside him. Nah, I wanted to *be* Larry Johnson! He calls me his little brother to this day.

The Runnin' Rebels were this unbelievable force. They played in the Big West Conference, so I was able to go to their away games at nearby Long Beach State and Cal State, Fullerton. Plus, they were always on TV. Between attending UNLV games and watching UNLV games on TV, I saw a ton of UNLV hoops and loved every minute of it. They changed the way people viewed basketball games—they made it a show before the game even started. They'd have this elaborate firework display and they'd

In my Artesia High School days.

put a spotlight on each player. They played in front of twenty thousand people and always sold out on the road.

The Vegas community also embraced them. In a city where everything is a show, the Runnin' Rebels were the biggest show in town and the biggest draw on the strip. On one recruiting visit, Stacey and Larry took me to see Siegfried and Roy at the Stardust Resort and Casino. We're sitting there and A-list celebrities keep swinging by to say hi to them like they're royalty.

One who stood out was Buster Douglas. He was fresh off his shocking upset of Mike Tyson to become the heavyweight champion of the world. He's on top of the world at that moment in his life. And I'm watching him embrace Stacey and Larry right in front of me like they're longtime friends. Then Julius Erving— Dr. J—sees Stacey and Larry...and *he* makes a beeline toward *them*. Then Stacey and Larry introduce me to him. I can't stop smiling. I'm getting to meet Dr. J. I was acting like a fanboy, but I couldn't help it.

Then it got even better. Dr. J tells me he has watched me play on TV and was really impressed by my game. "You've got an explosive first step, young man. Your lateral quickness also stands out. I like it." My jaw is on the floor. We're talking Dr. J. here. The same Dr. J who is one of the greatest basketball players of all time. The same Dr. J who is possibly the best small forward God ever created. The same Dr. J who made basketball fun with his insanely creative dunks and flair for dramatic plays. And, yes, the same Dr. J who is the star of my favorite B movie, *The Fish that Saved Pittsburgh*.

Playing for UNLV back then was like playing for Kentucky today: you must be a really good player. Their colors were even the same as my high school: black, red, and white. And their mascot, this mountain man with a huge mustache, Hey Reb, looked like ours. They even ran the same plays as my high school team. And I'd be lying if I said their cheerleaders weren't hot.

It was my destiny to go UNLV and help the program repeat as champions. They were going to become college basketball's dynasty team in the 1990s. UNLV wanted me, too. So did UCLA, USC, Louisiana State, Syracuse, and a bunch of other top programs. The kids at Arizona State even made WE WANT ED T-shirts, though we crossed that school off the list when, with my mom literally standing right next to me, one of their assistant basketball coaches told me, "We're rated by *Playboy* as the number-one party school in the country!" I smiled politely but then looked at my mom, who had this blank look on her face. What was that guy thinking?

Anyway, I was ranked the number-one college prospect in the country and schools were calling every day. It validated all of the hard work I had put into becoming a really good basketball player. My parents and Charles were so proud of me. But I only wanted to play at one school—UNLV—and in May 1990 I committed to playing there following high school graduation. A few months later, though, I reluctantly decommitted. In the process, I gained an unwanted introduction to the NCAA and their oppressive methods.

Let me set the scene. I knew about UNLV's problems with the NCAA because Coaches Tark and Grgurich were up-front about those problems. During one of his visits to my home, Coach Tark told me, "Ed, we'd love to have you, but we don't want you to sign a letter of intent." He was referring to a national letter of intent, or NLI, which is a binding pledge by a high school athlete to a college. If it is broken, the athlete has to sit out of college sports for an entire year. NLIs don't do much for the athlete. It's basically a one-way contract.

"We don't want you to feel the wrath of what's going on with the NCAA," Coach Tark explained. "I want you to be able to get out of this if we get hit with sanctions. Just give me your word, Ed—that's all we need. And for your own sake, please don't put it in writing." Now, when Coach Tark said that, I immediately wanted to put it all in writing. Here was a coach whom the NCAA made everyone believe was dishonest and deceitful, and yet he was doing me right against his own self-interest. It was really noble. It was something very different from what I had heard from other schools' coaches.

What the coaches were telling me wasn't a huge surprise. The NCAA had always seemed to be after UNLV, and especially Coach Tark. NCAA officials had alleged that UNLV gave what the NCAA likes to term "improper benefits"—money—to recruits. Coach Tark had a bullseye on his back. He had gone to court to fight the NCAA, and his legal efforts, as I understood them, stopped a suspension that the NCAA tried to impose on him in the late 1970s for stuff they said he did while coaching Long Beach State in the early 1970s. The NCAA just doesn't like to let go.

I also knew there was some lingering controversy from the mid-1980s when UNLV had recruited Lloyd Daniels, a talented guard from New York City who—as reported by the press including the *New York Times* and *Los Angeles Times*—ended up getting busted for drugs.

I'm not going to claim UNLV and its coaches were angels. Like other top basketball programs, they operated in a space where NCAA rules are often broken. And even if I supported his underlying motivations, Coach Tark openly defied rules that he and UNLV accepted. So, no, we're not talking about unclean hands here. I'm not on a mission to rehabilitate anyone or any school's mission. But whatever Coach Tark did or did not do, I am certain of two facts.

First, my palms never reached out "under the table" to anyone, and that's especially true when I was with Coach Tark. I badly wanted to go to UNLV. The last thing I needed was cash and gifts as inducements. Hell, if anything, I would have given up things to join the Runnin' Rebels. From my perspective, the deal for me to attend UNLV was sealed the moment UNLV expressed interest. That's how much I wanted to go there. Second, Coach Tark played the same game as other coaches. Coaches aren't necessarily corrupt. And, as my own experience shows, they aren't always corrupt. It's just that at times, coaches feel like they have no choice *but* to break rules. They know rival programs are doing the same. So it becomes the college sports version of keeping up with the Joneses.

Coaches aren't stupid, either. They know what they've been hired to do. A coach could be the greatest educator ever of student-athletes. He could have preacher-like inspirational qualities. He could be a father figure to young men who didn't have fathers. He could be all of that, but if he loses, he's out.

That's why this whole system is broken. The NCAA imposes rules that winning programs know they can't follow if they actually want to win. These rules make it impossible for coaches to be educators, even though they work for higher education institutions. At the end of the day, it is all—*totally all*—about winning.

That's not to say that we can always blame the system. There are coaches who go too far or, conversely, who do too little.

Take Rick Pitino. Pitino's removal from the Louisville head coaching job in October 2017 was a long time coming—as shown by incidents covered by the *New York Times, Washington Post, Louisville Courier-Journal*, and ESPN. First there was the accusation that he gave money and cars to a woman after having a sexual encounter with her in a local restaurant. Then we hear from Katrina Powell, the former escort who authored the book *Breaking Cardinal Rules: Basketball and the Escort Queen*, about hooker parties that she had organized for Louisville recruits in university dorms. Then we hear about $100,000 cash payments to five-star recruits.

My man, how many chances do you get?

Look, whether Pitino was directly involved in all or some of the scandals in his program, it doesn't really matter. He was the head of the program. Shame on him if he was directly involved. And shame on him if he didn't know. Pitino is also known as a control freak. It's a little hard to believe he had no idea. So from my vantage point, coaches have gotten fired over much less.

Take my college coach, Jim Harrick. About a year after I left UCLA for the NBA, Coach Harrick lost his job because—according to the *Los Angeles Times*, *Sports Illustrated*, and the *New York Times*, among others—he didn't list all of the food expenses he incurred while he and his wife dined with players and recruits. That's right. He lost his job over food! Until the NCAA passed a rule change in 2015 that lets schools provide unlimited meals to college athletes, schools were literally punished if they provided "too many" meals to athletes or if they let athletes have others buy them meals. If a food-related "offense" can warrant dismissal, then certainly Rick Pitino had used up his nine coaching lives.

But that doesn't justify what happened to Coach Tark. I didn't anticipate that a failed coaching suspension in the 1970s and a controversial recruiting effort in the 1980s would have any impact on high school students that UNLV was recruiting in the 1990s. And yet that is exactly what happened.

See, the NCAA believed that UNLV and Coach Tark were never properly punished. From there, the NCAA claimed that UNLV broke rules in how the school recruited me. I later learned that the NCAA was upset that I worked out with Larry Johnson and Stacey Augmon when I visited the UNLV campus. The NCAA was also angry that Larry and Stacey took me out to dinner and picked up the tab. These were so-called impermissible benefits in the eyes of NCAA officials, even though they were completely related to whether I would be a good fit at UNLV. Could you imagine the uproar if a UNLV history major paid for the dinner of a high school senior who was visiting UNLV on admitted students day and trying to learn more about the history program? Exactly. There would be none.

Despite the warning signs, I felt great about my pledge to join UNLV. That is, until I was in South America a couple of months later. It was July 21, 1990. I was in Montevideo, the capital city of Uruguay, as a member of the US national team playing in the FIBA Americas Under-18 Championship. After a game I headed back to my hotel room. I was there only a few minutes when I heard a loud knock.

It was Derrick Martin, our starting point guard and the starting point guard at UCLA. Derrick was a legend in the Los Angeles basketball world. He had starred at St. Anthony High School in Long Beach and was a McDonald's All-American. He'd later play thirteen seasons in the NBA. I smiled and greeted Derrick. "Hey, man, what's up?"

"You hear about UNLV?"

"Ahh, no, what happened?"

"You guys are going on probation!"

"Wait, what? When did that happen?"

"Just saw it on the news. Are you going to transfer?"

"I don't know. I don't know."

"Well what are you going to do?"

I obviously knew this was a possibility, but I was still stunned. And I was pissed off. I mean, what *could have been*, you know? We would have won for years at UNLV. They were other guys, like me, in the pipeline—rumor was even a couple of the "Fab 5" were going to join the program instead of Michigan until the sanctions hit.

But when the NCAA wants to stop something, they stop it. And they don't care about any collateral damage to kids like me who had done nothing wrong. There's a reason why people believe the NCAA going after UNLV and Coach Tark was a conspiracy.

After Derrick left, I called my dad, and he confirmed the

news. "We have a lot to talk about when you get home, Ed." Indeed we did.

And when I got back to LA, my parents and I spoke with Coach Tark and Coach Grg. They explained exactly what was going on. They said the NCAA was going to put UNLV on probation for two years. I was a seventeen-year-old kid and didn't really know what probation meant. But as the coaches told me, it meant that UNLV was going to be barred from appearing on TV and in tournaments. These restrictions would hurt the program and its players, especially those, like me, who could have NBA careers.

"How does the NCAA have the power to stop teams from appearing on TV?" I asked Coach Tark and Coach Grg, and my dad, too. "What kind of association is this?"

There were no good answers.

Instead, Coach Grg said to me, "As much as we want you to be here, Ed, and as much as we know you want to be here, it wouldn't be right for you. You and Shon deserve better." Shon Tarver was one of my best friends from Santa Clara High School. He was another UNLV recruit, and he was just as bummed as I was.

So that was the end of my association with UNLV. It was short and unsweet. The NCAA had wronged me, and it was largely over how closely Coach Tark followed unfair amateurism rules way back in the early 1970s, before I was even born. Crazy.

I called Jim Harrick, UCLA's coach, to set up an unofficial visit and walk around the campus. I visited and signed a letter of intent to join the Bruins. Shon picked UCLA as well, and we ended up being roommates there.

After I switched my commitment to UCLA, I thought I was done with the NCAA and its investigations. They got what they wanted: the destruction of a dynasty and the downfall of a good man.

Kindergarten

Eleventh

First

Tenth

Second

Ninth

Third

Senior

Eighth

Fourth

Seventh

Fifth

Sixth

From kindergarten through high school.

I was wrong.

In the summer of 1990, before I started my freshman year at UCLA, I was working out with Shon and other Bruins players in the gym. After finishing up, I went to the locker room, where a UCLA official rushed over to Shon and me to tell us that we needed to talk to NCAA investigators ASAP. We asked him what this was about and he said he couldn't tell us. We figured it was about UNLV.

We hadn't showered. We hadn't changed. We hadn't eaten. We had no opportunity to prepare our thoughts or come up with a statement. We weren't given time to talk to a lawyer if that idea had come to us (it didn't—don't forget, we were just teenagers and not even college freshmen yet). Our parents obviously weren't with us at the time, either.

We had no one but ourselves—two teenage kids who were tall in height but short on wisdom. Naturally, we felt really intimidated. You might call it powerless. We believed we had no choice but to meet with these NCAA guys.

Minutes later, while Shon and I are still wearing basketball gear, we're meeting in a room with four middle-aged dudes wearing suits. They start grilling me with questions about whether Coach Tark had given me gifts and whether I was paid in my recruiting visit to UNLV. They tried to find inconsistencies in what I said, but I had none. They asked me hypotheticals, hoping to trip me up. I just told the truth. The whole time, I was thinking, *Who the hell are these guys? Is this the FBI?*

When I got back to my dorm room, I realized how aggressive these guys really were—there were multiple messages on my answering machine about how the NCAA was in town and how they needed to talk to me.

So for teenagers like Shon and me, "amateurism" meant having to meet with investigators at unannounced visits and without the benefit of advice or counsel from our parents, let alone lawyers. It was totally oppressive and completely inappropriate.

Worse yet, the NCAA dragged my name through the mud. In July, the *Los Angeles Times* ran a story on the front page of the sports section with the all-caps headline O'BANNON'S VEGAS TRIP SCRUTINIZED. The story was about a plane ticket UNLV had given me and how, "according to sources"—I wonder who they might be?—my dad and I told the NCAA that we didn't know who paid for the plane ticket. They made it sound like we had done something criminal.

Why would I have paid for a plane ticket when it was to visit a school that was recruiting me? The recruiting school—and not the recruited high school student or his parents—should pay for it. But this is what the NCAA does: it leaks stories to the media to paint others as the bad guys.

Being interrogated by NCAA officials wasn't the only experience at UCLA that made me question what the NCAA does in its strange world of amateurism. Even seemingly trivial events brought those rules into focus.

It was May of 1991. Shon and I were regularly playing pickup ball with a bunch of guys who were in their twenties. One of them worked for the Lakers in ticket sales. I'll call him Tim. Tim had played high school ball years earlier and was a big fan of UCLA hoops. As a gift, Tim gave Shon and me tickets to watch game one of the Lakers–Golden State Warriors playoff series at the Forum in Inglewood.

That was awesome. I was a huge Showtime fan.

I don't mean Showtime the cable channel, although it is a solid channel, to be sure. I'm talking about the period of the time when the Lakers redefined NBA basketball. That period became known as *Showtime*.

In the 1980s and early '90s, the Lakers played an unprecedented, up-tempo style that other teams would soon mimic.

For decades NBA teams had typically used half-court sets with drawn-out plays. Showtime changed that. It was about pushing the ball up the court as fast as possible, fearlessly driving to the hoop, and using dazzling passes to overwhelm opponents. Magic Johnson, Kareem Abdul-Jabbar, James Worthy, Michael Cooper, and Byron Scott were amazing. I wanted to be like them and loved it when people compared my game to that of Worthy.

Although Showtime was winding down by 1991—Abdul-Jabbar had already retired and Pat Riley had moved on to coach the Knicks—I couldn't turn down a chance to see the Lakers play, especially a playoff game. Lakers tickets were also really expensive and always in demand. In a celebrity town where it means a lot for one's reputation to be seen in certain places, going to a Lakers home game back in the '80s and '90s always made someone look cool.

For their part, the Warriors were pretty incredible back then as well. This was their "Run TMC" era, when Tim Hardaway, Mitch Richmond, and Chris Mullin played a run-and-gun style that was both high scoring and extremely entertaining. Now, don't get me wrong: the Warriors of the '90s weren't as good as the Warriors of today, with Stephen Curry, Kevin Durant, Klay Thompson, and Draymond Green leading the way. But Run TMC were damn good in their own right.

It was an awesome matchup and Shon and I were psyched. We could never afford to go to Lakers games and yet now had secured Lakers playoff tickets.

But for a brief moment, an annoying thought crossed our minds: would accepting tickets from a guy who works for an NBA team run afoul of NCAA amateurism rules and get us in trouble? The NCAA prohibits "gifts" to student-athletes, although that rule is intended to regulate agents and boosters. As far as we knew, Tim wasn't an agent. Whether he was a "booster"—which the NCAA defines as a "representative of the institution's athletic interests"—was less clear. He seemed to be a UCLA fan, but we had no reason to believe he donated money to UCLA or promoted the school, just as we had no information that he recruited athletes to attend UCLA or provided jobs or internships to UCLA athletes.

The thought passed quickly. We broke our backs for college sports and did so without getting paid a dime. Going to a Lakers game for free shouldn't be a worry. And so we went to the game. We had a blast, too. The seats were a few rows behind the court and we saw Magic score a triple double in a high-scoring Lakers win.

A couple of days later Tim gave us tickets to game two. As much as Shon and I wanted to go, another thought crossed our minds. We were eyeing a chance to eat at a fancy Chinese restaurant right near the UCLA campus. It was one of those restaurants that, if you looked it up on Yelp nowadays, would have four dollar-sign icons. It was real pricey. But a number of our classmates dined there and loved it. Unlike those classmates, we didn't have spending money for that kind of dining. We weren't alone. Most players on Division I basketball and football teams rely almost exclusively on university meal plans for food. Look at the income and wealth of parents of student-athletes versus that for parents of other students—it will tell you a lot about college sports and why amateurism is so problematic.

So instead of attending game two of the series, we decided to scalp the tickets and go watch the game on TV—after a delicious Chinese meal, of course. We picked up the tickets at the Forum's will call window and walked over to the adjacent street. We heard a guy yelling, "Tickets? Tickets? Buying? Selling?"

We didn't know if selling our tickets was legal. We also didn't know if this guy was an undercover cop. There also seemed to be a better-than-average chance that we might be recognized. After all, I'm six foot eight and Shon is six foot six. And we look like basketball players...basketball players scalping basketball tickets!

We sold the tickets for face value and sprinted to our car. We then drove to the Chinese restaurant, where we completely pigged out. General Tso's chicken. Noodles. Fried rice. You name it. Then we watched the game on TV back at our dorm.

Did we follow NCAA rules with those Lakers tickets? I'm not sure. But we wanted to live like other UCLA students and we weren't going to let NCAA rules stand in our way.

So, yeah, maybe my parents are proud of me for taking on the NCAA in court. It's one thing to be known as a talented athlete. It's another to be known as a fighter for justice.

I'll take the latter.

CHAPTER 8

THE MANY WAYS OF VALUING COLLEGE ATHLETES' IDENTITIES

Throughout the trial, it was painfully obvious that the NCAA's witnesses didn't want to be there. In fact, it seemed like they were offended to have to answer questions about their system of amateurism—like it was beneath them to talk to my lawyers about athlete compensation. I also got the impression that they were trying to make our case less significant than it actually was. They didn't want to be on the hook if they lost what the rest of the sports world viewed as a historic case.

Plus, at least from where I was sitting—and, hey, I had a pretty good seat—most of the NCAA witnesses were smug about their chances. It seemed like they believed that they would win no matter what happened in the trial, all because they had the mighty "NCAA" across their jerseys.

It's all too bad, really. If NCAA officials weren't so darn arrogant, they could have changed amateurism rules long before I sued them. They never would have wound up in court. They never would have had to sit on a witness stand trying to defend a peculiar system to a federal judge who was no sports fan and clearly viewed the NCAA with a skeptical eye.

But that's not the NCAA mentality. To them, to defend the system is all that matters. Even if that system is obviously flawed and undoubtedly unfair, the NCAA operates in a space where dissent simply isn't tolerated.

While all of the NCAA witnesses were memorable for one reason or another, there was one who really stuck out to me: Bernard Muir, the athletic director at Stanford University. A black man in his mid-forties and a former college basketball player at Brown University, Muir gave the most memorable witness testimony in the trial. From my vantage point, his answers undermined the NCAA's central argument for amateurism.

Initially, Muir framed the debate as one in which a plaintiff's victory would make college athletes too focused on the almighty dollar and uninterested in academics. "If we go down that path to paying for name, image, and likeness," Muir testified, "that takes away from why our students are there, for the education. The focus could be on driving resources in that regard and that would concern me." When he said that, I remember shaking my head in disbelief. I was grinning slightly, too.

The position Muir was advocating was one I totally disagreed with. Does he really believe that compensating a college student for using his or her identity would interfere with that student's learning? How so? What is that fear based on? Is the student suddenly going to stop attending class when he receives a little extra money because he's in a video game or on TV broadcast? You'd think the NCAA would be more worried about the educational impact of college athletes spending fifty hours a week on sports than whether those athletes are compensated for the use of their identities. Logic would bring you there. But logic and the NCAA often don't go hand in hand.

For that matter, I wondered, did Muir have the same worry when Stanford student Reese Witherspoon got compensated for the use of her name, image, and likeness in movies and TV shows? And was he concerned when Stanford students Fred Savage and Ben Savage capitalized on the use of their identities in *The Wonder Years* and *Boy Meets World*? Or how about when Muir was a student at Brown in the late 1980s and his classmate, Lisa Loeb, was a well-known professional musician at the time? Did it bother him that what made Loeb's voice and songwriting valuable benefited her, just as it benefited record companies and her bandmates?

The value of a college athlete's image isn't only found in obvious places like video games and TV broadcasts. Sometimes it surfaces when the athlete isn't even being shown. Let me—and my recent knee replacement—explain.

We know the NCAA often insists that college athletes and college students are basically the same: they're all college students! This "big tent" mentality is misleading on a number of levels, some of which are instantly recognizable and some of which aren't.

• • •

It happened around 8 p.m. on Tuesday, October 9, 1990.

I remember everything.

I was an eighteen-year-old freshman at the time. But I wasn't just any freshman. I was the most highly recruited freshman in college basketball and I was playing on a team that had a legitimate shot to win the national championship. Can it get any better? The whole world seemed in front of me, like I was the star of a movie that began when my parents gave me a basketball to hold as a toddler and I wouldn't let it go. Everything had been moving in the direction of my becoming a star player.

And it seemed like the world was watching this movie, too.

Along with Kareem Abdul-Jabbar, Bill Walton, and Don MacLean, I had just been photographed to grace the cover of *Sports Illustrated*'s 1990 college basketball preview issue. *SI* predicted that Don—who was a few years ahead of me and was one of the sweetest shooters I've ever seen—and I would help UCLA return to the glory days of Abdul-Jabbar and Walton. The thought of being on the cover of *Sports Illustrated* before I had even started playing college basketball was almost crazy.

As it turned out, it was too crazy. I'd be removed from the photo before the *Sports Illustrated* issue ran. And it all had to do with what took place on the evening of October 9, 1990.

We were still a week away from practices, but my teammates and I had been working out regularly and playing pickup basketball games at the Wooden Center. We attracted some decent-sized crowds, too. I knew the fans were there at least in part to watch Shon Tarver and me—the two big recruits—play. Bruins fans were dreaming of an NCAA title.

Back then I was a high-jumping player with a crazy vertical leap. I could literally touch the top of the backboard—sometimes higher! I didn't quite have Michael Jordan's hops, but leaping was a big part of my game. It was a major way coaches and fans distinguished me from other six-foot-eight power forwards. It allowed me to drive to the hoop and explode over players. This was true even of players who were a few inches taller than me: with my leap, I could get higher than them in midair and my strength allowed me to get separation. Coaches taught me to develop my game to take full advantage of this skillset.

And, oh yeah, I could do some crazy dunks back then!

Well, that night we had been playing pickup for a while. Our games were up to 11 by 1s, but at some point things started to get sloppy. Guys were really tired and lost focus. What seemed like our last game came to an end. We should have called it a night.

I wish we had.

Instead, we wanted to finish the night strong and leave on a good note. *Let's just play one more game* was the consensus view.

So we started to play that last game. I was playing defense and positioned off the ball. I saw Don MacLean cut for a pass. Mitchell Butler was dribbling up the court at the time. It was one of those plays where my man came off a pick down low and popped out to the wing. I read the play from beginning to end. Mitchell was going to throw the pass to Don on the pick and roll. Immediately before Mitchell attempted to throw that pass, I jumped into the passing lane and stole the ball from him. I had timed it perfectly.

At that moment, the only thing standing between the basket and me was about seventy feet of maple-wood floor. I had a straight, uncontested line to the hoop.

It was close to 8 p.m. and the crowd was pretty small. So what did that tell me about the people who were still there? These were the real diehard fans!

And they were watching me.

So maybe I wanted to give them a reward for their loyalty. Or maybe I just wanted to show off my hops. Either way, I wish I had had something else on my mind.

As I'm dribbling down the floor, I'm thinking in my head, *What would get the loudest oohs and ahhs from the crowd?* And the choice was completely mine. When you're playing in a pickup game and a player is on a breakaway, there's an unwritten rule that no one chases him down. He gets a clear lane to the hoop to do whatever he wants.

Whatever *I* want.

So as I'm dribbling full speed, I make my decision: go up and get my head as close to the rim as possible and then slam it home. A truly massive dunk that would show the world what they were getting in Ed O'Bannon.

It was a completely unnecessary move in a completely meaningless game. It was just showtime basketball.

Let me begin with the good news: two points.

The bad news? Everything else.

For some reason, I came down at an angle that was a little bit off. And just a little bit off can make all the difference in the world. I landed awkwardly and immediately felt a jolt in my left knee. What's crazy about it is that it didn't hurt. It just felt weird. And then I couldn't put weight on it. So I started to skip a bit and I noticed that my left leg was bent inward, like I was trying to kick. Except that...I wasn't trying to kick.

Deep down, right at that moment, I knew that I had completely torn up my knee.

But closer to the surface, I didn't want to admit it.

So my instinct was to make everything seem normal again as soon as possible. I then jumped on my right leg and I snapped my left leg back into place while doing that.

Then I decided to lie down on the court. And that was when it really hit me.

I looked up at the arena's ceiling and noticed the UCLA banners, but that's not what I saw.

I saw my career flash in front of my eyes. I thought my life was over at that moment. Everything that I had accomplished seemed liked the work of someone else: pre-injury Ed O'Bannon. Everything that had made me a special player I feared I would no longer be able to do. And those big dreams—leading UCLA to a national title? Taking on Charles Barkley and Karl Malone in the NBA? Gone. Instead of a bright future I saw just a dark abyss.

And it was all because of an ill-advised dunk in a game that meant nothing.

Everyone came running over to me. Derrick Martin. Gerald Watkins. Don MacLean. Shon Tarver. Mitchell Butler. I recognized their voices, but I had shut my eyes and put my hands over my eyes, so I couldn't see them.

They were reassuring—"Hey, Ed, you're okay, man, you'll be fine"—but they also seemed to recognize the gravity of the situation. They first wanted to carry me out on a stretcher. I said no. Then they suggested they would send for a wheelchair. I said absolutely not. Then they wanted to have me skip out on my good leg and use their shoulders as crutches to balance out the weight.

No thanks.

I told myself, *Ed, you* must *walk, no matter what.* No one was going to convince me otherwise.

So I stood up and told everyone that I felt okay and that I thought it was just a sprain—all of which, of course, I knew wasn't true. I waved off their help and just smiled, trying to make everyone there feel okay. I did end up walking—yes, walking—to the training room to try to prove to myself that it wasn't as bad as I knew it was. The training room, though, was not that close. It was in a different building, about a quarter of a mile away.

I did the best I could not to limp on that walk. I was being trailed by my teammates, people from the crowd, and curious onlookers, many of whom looked distraught. I was the prized recruit and badly injured. If all of this had happened nowadays, there'd already be videos and gifs of me on Twitter getting injured. Hashtags #OBannondown and #kneeblown. And later there would be videos of me hobbling on this walk. And I'm sure you could find the whole sequence in one of those "gruesome athlete injuries" videos on YouTube.

The walk mercifully came to an end. I landed on the training table with what seemed like a dozen UCLA doctors and trainers standing around me. They examined my leg in every way possible. I didn't know what they were looking for. But I knew what *I* was looking for—their facial reactions.

And not one had a positive expression. To be honest, it looked like they had seen a ghost.

By this point it was around 9 p.m. The doctors sent me home to my mom and dad's house. I had never before felt so devastated, so destroyed. The last time my parents had seen me they thought their son might one day become an NBA star. This time, I feared, they'd look at me like a has-been before I ever was.

But my parents aren't like that. They'd love me with no leg, let alone an injured one. And that was how they received me that night.

The next day—Wednesday—I went into UCLA Medical Center for an MRI. Dr. David Grauer, the orthopedic surgeon, evaluated the results and then calmly and sorrowfully told me what had happened: I had badly torn my anterior cruciate ligament (ACL) and meniscus cartilage in my left knee, and also chipped the bone. The medical team told me it was one of the most catastrophic knee injuries they had ever seen.

No doubt, I found the news distressing. However, I sort of figured it was coming. I knew the injury was really awful, so hearing the doctor confirm my instinct was not a huge surprise.

For the basketball world, though, it seemed like a tragedy. In fact, by Thursday my injury had become national news. I remember picking up a copy of the *Los Angeles Times* and the front page of the sports section had an article ominously titled, "O'Bannon Suffers Knee Injury, Will Have Surgery and Miss the Season." The article basically published my medical diagnosis, and it also had quotes from Don MacLean and others who had seen the injury. The writer also spoke with Assistant Coach Steve Lavin on what my injury meant for the team's chances.

Look, I wasn't upset at all by the article—I knew media coverage was part of the territory of being a well-known Division I athlete. But I had just turned eighteen and was in the first semester of my freshman year in college. Would the same injury to one of my fellow freshmen have been in the newspaper? Would the school even have allowed his or her medical condition to become public?

I then had to decide how we would repair the injury. The doctors recommended that I get an assist from a cadaver.

My father had learned of a new procedure that hadn't been perfected but would give me a chance for a complete recovery. When a ligament is as severely torn as mine was, it's almost impossible to fully repair it. And even if the repair is perfect, a reconstructed ACL is vulnerable to reinjury, especially when exposed to the kind of continuous and demanding physical activity that a basketball player endures. So doctors had devised a procedure in which they replace a badly damaged ACL with a healthy ligament from the Achilles tendon of another person. The new ACL is much stronger than a repaired ACL and is much more durable. The new ACL is also more likely to hold the knee in place and feel similar to the way it was before the injury.

This made a lot of sense to my parents and me.

Living people, though, aren't giving up their Achilles tendons, so the donor is a cadaver. Some of my friends were a little freaked out about the idea of my getting a dead person's body part, but it didn't faze me at all. I was totally focused on making a full recovery and, realistically, the only way I'd be able to do that was through the transplant. Instead of feeling weird about getting a cadaver's body part, I felt grateful that such a procedure existed. I also felt blessed that there are generous people out there who sign up as organ donors before they pass on.

Surgery day was on Thursday, October 18—nine very long and very frustrating days after the injury occurred. The procedure would last more than five hours. I unexpectedly woke up in the middle of it and felt totally disoriented—I had no idea where I was. I remember that the doctor looked at me and was kind of stunned that I had woken up. I was like, "What's up, doc?" He told me, "You're in the middle of your surgery." He then gave me a choice: "Ed, if you look over to your left you can watch the rest of the procedure. Or we can put you back to sleep if you like." I looked over and there was a little monitor. On it, I could see inside my knee, guts and all. "Ahh, doctor, I'd like to be put back to sleep, thank you."

The recovery process felt like it took forever. I took the rest of the year off academically and basically moved back into my parents' house. I'd go to all the home games but not the road games. For the first two months I wasn't allowed to put any pressure on my leg. But I worked into a routine where I'd spend all day in the training room and then go home.

I hated having to go back home. I obviously love my parents and love my home, but being in that situation—I absolutely hated it. I was separated from the one thing that gives any player comfort: being with your teammates and your brothers. As soon as you get injured, you are your own person. Even if you want to remain with the team, you really can't. You and your teammates have different schedules, different expectations, and different goals. Everything is different. You're not part of the group anymore, no matter how much they and you try to restore the way things were.

And I had adjusted really well to college life. Hanging out with my buddies, living in a dorm, playing basketball, learning from great professors, going to parties—you name it. Those were good times. For that part of my life to end so drastically and to suddenly be back in the bedroom I grew up in except with only one good leg this time—it was very humbling and dispirit-ing. Really, I never did get used to it. And being honest, I wasn't a happy person to be around. I'm sure my parents would tell you that.

Speaking of my parents, they refused to tell me how nervous they were about whether I would recover, but I could tell that they were very concerned. I can't tell you how many times my dad would tell me, "I wish the injury happened to me instead of you." They were scared. Confused. The whole bit. As a father of three, I can tell you there's nothing worse than when your child gets hurt. Parental protection kicks in real fast.

In the spring semester I moved back to the dorms, which psychologically helped out a lot. I felt like I was back to where I belonged. I didn't take classes and couldn't practice, but my recovery was going well. I trained like a machine—I would get to the training room in the morning and not leave until late in the day. I was extremely focused. While my legs recovered through physical therapy, I improved other parts of my body—chest, shoulders, arms, and abs. I used the recovery process to become a lot stronger.

I had a lot of support in my recovery, including from com-plete strangers. It's kind of crazy how my injury and recovery were topics of newspaper articles and ESPN reports. I remember getting a get-well card from Paula Abdul and I got one from Michael Jackson, too. The best may have been a phone call from Kareem Abdul-Jabbar. The sports information director at UCLA, Bill Bennett, had given me a heads up that Kareem would be calling at a particular day and time. I told my best friend (and future best man), Leroy, about it and he begged me to be able to answer the phone when Kareem called. I let him.

Man, what a thrill it was to speak with Kareem. I grew up a diehard Lakers fan, so it was one of the greatest thrills to have a one-on-one conversation with him. I remember he told me, "My brother, the city of Los Angeles is behind you. You will come out of this better than before." I was in the dumps, so it made me feel good.

Celebrities weren't the only ones who reached out to me. Tons of strangers wrote me letters saying they were pulling for me. These were from people of all ages, races, and backgrounds. Some were UCLA grads. Others were kids who admired my game. And still others were older folks who told me that life is long and not to worry.

I was incredibly thankful for all the concern people had for me. But think about it for a minute. How often does a typical college student or even a typical college athlete get that kind of attention? I'm sure there were other UCLA students who suffered similarly serious injuries around the same time as me and my guess is they didn't get letters from Michael Jackson. Don't get me wrong—I genuinely appreciated the support. Seriously. But ask yourself: why did people care so much about my injury and recovery?

For some, I'm sure they heard the news and felt really bad for me. But it's hard to deny the larger situation. I was considered crucial to UCLA's chances for a national championship. And a lot of people cared deeply about those championship aspirations. Some even had reputational and financial stakes in them.

So, I was not at all like other students with a similar injury. To me, this experience is more evidence that the NCAA's depiction of amateurism—that it ensures that college athletes are treated the same as other college students—isn't grounded in reality. My injury was newsworthy not because it involved UCLA student Ed O'Bannon. It was newsworthy because it involved UCLA basketball player Ed O'Bannon.

It took a long time to recover. While I was completely confident that I'd return, I was also aware that a lot of basketball players who suffered ACL injuries never came back. And some of those who did return were never the same. For some, their games changed. Tim Hardaway, for example, lost some of the electric quality that made him so dynamic. He still found a way to excel, but more with outside shooting than dunking over defenders. However, I found optimism in Bernard King's ACL injury and his recovery. He was an amazing player both before and after his ACL injury.

I started to play again during the summer of 1991. I took it slow and was very tentative. I would spend the '91–92 year as a redshirt freshman. It was basically a rehab year. The doctors and coaching staff determined that I could only play in limited stints, so, five or ten minutes a game. By '92–93 I was back to playing full time, and statistically I had a very good year—I averaged seventeen points and seven rebounds a game. But psychologically it was an experimental year for me in that I was discovering what I could and couldn't do. I was trying really hard to regain my confidence.

I also began to adapt as a player during that '92–93 season. Whereas I used to drive to the bucket all the time, I didn't have the same conviction to do that anymore, at least not so frequently. So, my game evolved. I became more of a jump shooter on the wing. I continued to play that way in the '93–94 season but regained some of my confidence in driving to the hoop. This was also around the time I felt that the range of motion in my knee was mostly back. It wasn't the same as before, but it felt like it was getting there.

In truth, I never fully recovered from the knee injury. There was just too much damage for the body to take. I would say I got back 90 percent of my athleticism. I became a different player. It all worked out, but I still regret that dunk.

On the bright side, I learned a lot about overcoming obstacles. And I learned how even injuries test the believability of amateurism.

• • •

Twenty-two years later, as I listened to Bernard Muir on the witness stand in Judge Wilken's courtroom, the believability of amateurism continued to confound me. I couldn't help but be stunned by the statements of this man, *the* athletic director of Stanford University, one of the most academically rigorous universities in the country. It seemed more than a little odd to hear such a distinguished man from such a distinguished institution opine that compensating a college athlete for the use of his identity would hurt his education yet compensating other college students—be they actors, musicians, or anyone else—for their identities wouldn't. His position just didn't make any sense to me.

Muir made other head-scratching remarks. He suggested that he didn't know where all of the money would come from if college athletes were paid for the use of their identities.

Right.

The NCAA, which generates nearly $1 billion a year in revenue, is apparently impoverished. I guess the same goes for Stanford University, which has an endowment of merely $22 billion. I really don't know where the money would come from—everyone is broke!

Muir also echoed the testimony of University of South Carolina president Harris Pastides, who had testified for the NCAA right before Muir took the stand. Pastides warned Judge Wilken that college athletes who don't receive "rewards"—notice the word Pastides used there—for the NCAA's use of their names, images, and likenesses would become "second-class citizens" and would "feel worse about themselves."

First off, who knew that being paid what one is rightfully owed is a "reward"? Payment isn't a gift when it reflects what you've earned. Second, the NCAA, which doesn't let someone buy a cup a coffee for a college athlete but lets that same person buy a cup of coffee or even a whole meal for the athlete's classmates, is really worried about college athletes "feeling worse" about themselves? And third, when did we ever say that because some college athletes would receive money other athletes wouldn't? We never made that argument.

This basic NCAA theory—that college athletes would be hurt if they were compensated for the use of their names, images, and likenesses—didn't hold up too well when Muir was cross-examined by Renae Steiner, one of our lawyers.

Renae picked him apart. It was beautiful how she did it.

After Muir praised his athletic program for compliance with NCAA rules, Renae showed him pictures of Stanford football players that the university was selling on its website (of course, none of the revenue goes to those players).

Oops. Muir said he would look into it and report it to the NCAA. Guess you kind of have to once it comes up in a trial.

Later during cross-examination, Muir admitted that the system of amateurism *wouldn't* be threatened by any and all payments for the use of college athletes' names, images, and likenesses. He thought that college athletes receiving six or seven figures would jeopardize amateurism, but then implied that five figures probably wouldn't. In other words, Muir contradicted the NCAA's defense that the only way to separate college sports from pro sports is to enforce a bright-line rule where *no figure* is paid to college athletes.

Then, toward the end of Muir's testimony, he basically acknowledged that what the NCAA and its members do is bad for college athletes, but that it's necessary to enforce bad rules because they've always been there. And, of course, these are rules that NCAA administrators financially benefit from.

Muir helped me cement my thoughts about the system and why it needed to change. The system is amateurism for the players, but not for the enterprise itself. And there are plenty of NCAA, conference, and college athletic executives who profit handsomely from this system.

And, look, I get that it may have been more difficult for him to testify given that he was a fellow black guy. I'm sure it's awkward to be up there trying to defend a system that takes a lot more from black kids than it does white ones. But his race doesn't mean he was willing to risk his job.

I felt there was no way we would lose after Muir stepped down from the witness stand. It was game over.

And sure enough, Judge Wilken would cite Muir's comments in ruling for us. She wrote, "Muir similarly acknowledged that his concerns about paying student-athletes varied depending on the size of the payments that they would receive" and that he "indicated that smaller payments to student-athletes would bother [him] less than larger payments."

Indeed.

CHAPTER 9

JUDGING THE JUDGE

The Honorable Claudia Ann Wilken was the real star of the trial. She was unfailingly fair and evenhanded the entire time. I couldn't have been more impressed.

Having never been in a trial, I didn't know what to expect from the judge. All I could do was go by what I had seen in movies and on TV. Judges are often depicted as going out of their way to make it clear that they're in charge. They have a scowl on their face, with one arm on the desk, the other arm on their hip, all the while leaning forward with an inquisitive look. They appear stern and uncompromising, the kind of people who make others feel nervous and fearful.

Judge Wilken wasn't like that at all. There was no drama and little tension over the three weeks. She was calm. She was straightforward. She never tried to intimidate. She simply commanded the room and earned the respect of the people in it.

I particularly liked that Judge Wilken was not a sports fan. She clearly knew little about college sports and the many layers to it. Compensation for coaches, how teams are selected for postseason play, the Bowl system—all of it and more were unfamiliar territory for her.

To her credit Judge Wilken admitted as much. At times she mixed up conference names, calling the Pac-12 the Pac-10, and then corrected herself. She also joked that, in her usual world, the phrase "the SEC" means the Securities and Exchange Commission, not the Southeastern Conference. At other times she didn't seem to know where teams played or to which school a team nickname referred. A reference to John Calipari and Pete Carroll would mean nothing to her.

Some people sitting in the court—including several journalists—snickered and rolled their eyes. The sense I got was that they believed Judge Wilken's lack of sports knowledge somehow discredited her. I completely disagreed. Judge Wilken not knowing about sports forced everyone in the trial to be really specific about what they were talking about. Nobody could make any assumptions that Judge Wilken knew more than what they were actually saying. And sometimes when people have to explain what they would otherwise assume is known in a conversation, those assumptions don't sound as convincing or secure.

For that reason, Judge Wilken reminded me of Rosa, a bit. Neither of them knew much about the industry but they could both see something was profoundly wrong.

Judge Wilken wasn't a fan of any team and so she wasn't invested in maintaining the status quo. The NCAA waxing poetic and romanticizing about college sports would do nothing to lead Judge Wilken astray. In fact, if college sports were radically different tomorrow—or even if college sports disappeared altogether tomorrow—Judge Wilken's life would be exactly the same as it is right now.

Judge Wilken could read between the lines, if you will. She could sense something was amiss, even if it didn't scream out as such. Even if it didn't want to admit what it really was.

This I could relate to all too well.

• • •

Before our case got as big as it did, several people reached out to me about college assistant coaching positions and TV color commentating opportunities. I later became a candidate for some of those jobs. But once those potential employers found out that I had this lawsuit against the NCAA and saw that the case was progressing toward a trial, those opportunities fell off the map. One potential employer even told me that because I was suing the NCAA, "We don't want to touch you."

Let me give you a few examples.

In 2010 I received a phone call from an agent I didn't even know. He told me that a college conference was interested in my doing TV color commentary for their men's basketball games. I responded that I'd love to do it. We talked about recording my trial commentary of a game and how I would train for it. It was very exciting. I enjoy talking about the game and I believe my insights would be informative to viewers.

A couple of days later, however, the agent called me back and said, "Hey, Ed, so you're suing the NCAA, huh?"

"Yeah, that's right."

I had assumed he knew that before he called me the first time. I'm sure he wishes he had.

"Look, Ed, the conference did a background check on you and Googled you. They read all about the lawsuit. The thing is, they don't want to bring on someone who is suing the NCAA. It puts them in an awkward spot. You understand, right?"

Oh yeah, I understood. I understood that I was being black-balled. When I told Rosa about this, she was angry. Here was a very good opportunity that had been taken away from us because of our case. But that's what we signed up for. It is what it is.

As disappointed as I was about the TV job, it was the denial of coaching jobs that really ticked me off.

In April 2011, Mark Gottfried took over as head coach of North Carolina State. I knew Mark well. He had been an assistant coach at UCLA when I played there. He always told me it would be great to coach together one day. Our respect for each other was mutual—Mark had taught me a great deal as my coach. I also connected really well with him on a personal level. It was like we had a bond.

I remember the day. Rosa and I were in Washington State at one of Little Ed's baseball games—by this point in time, Ed was quite the ballplayer and was on traveling teams in preparation for college baseball programs recruiting him. Mark told me how excited he was about his new job at NC State. It had been two years since he'd coached at the University of Alabama, which had let him go in the middle of a losing season. He seemed genuinely grateful to have another chance to be a head coach. I congratulated him and told him that he had paid his dues and earned it.

"Hey, Ed, what have you been up to?" I told Mark that I was leaving the following day to go back to school in LA. "Wow, that's great," Mark replied. I could hear the excitement in his voice. Later in the conversation, Mark asked me if I was interested in coaching. I enthusiastically replied, "YES."

"Let's keep in touch," Mark responded. "And let me know when you graduate and I'll have a spot for you, even if I have to create one. I want you on my staff." I was so pumped. Talk about a motivation to study and get my degree done! "To partner up with you would be amazing," I told Mark. "Count me in."

I had promised my mom that I'd go back to UCLA and finish my degree, and now my new educational mission had a second purpose. And the combined goal wasn't an easy one to accomplish. Each week I would drive six hours from Henderson, Nevada, to Los Angeles and stay at my parents' house, take a full load of classes, and then drive back six hours and work at Findlay on the weekend. In any spare time I would do my homework and study for quizzes and exams. I did this every week for an entire academic year. It was a really challenging experience, not only for me but also for my family and especially Rosa, who while working a full-time job watched the kids by herself with me out of town. Still, this was now about becoming a college coach. That purpose made it all worthwhile—or at least it should have.

Don't get me wrong—I enjoyed my job at Findlay and I enjoyed selling cars. I love the people I work with there to this day. But I've always known basketball—living it, breathing it. For years I'd go to games and scan the gym. I could identify the few kids who had a shot from the many who didn't. I knew the ones who were peaking in the eighth grade and the ones whose best days were ahead of them.

I also knew that I could be a strong mentor. I'm a dad and my kids are everything to me. I'm devoted to those who rely on my advice and counsel. Rosa and my kids agreed and gave their enthusiastic support. They told me they would follow me wherever my coaching career went.

In the months that followed, Mark and I kept in touch. I closely followed how NC State was playing and offered Mark my thoughts. I also let Mark know of my degree progress. He was very encouraging. In March 2012 Mark invited me to meet with him and others from NC State at the Final Four, which would be played at the Mercedes-Benz Superdome in New Orleans.

He told me the meeting would essentially be an interview and that it would be a mere formality. "All we have to do is this interview, Ed."

So I flew from Vegas to New Orleans and attended the Final Four. I watched the games closely, as mentally I was preparing to become an assistant coach at NC State. Then, after the University of Kentucky won the championship, Mark and I had lunch.

I thought the lunch would be the interview that Mark had promised. I thought we would finalize a deal for me to join the staff. I thought we would talk about Wolfpack players, strategy, and recruiting.

Instead, it was just lunch.

We sat at the table together and the waitress poured waters as we scanned the menus. Mark then looked up from the menu and made direct eye contact with me. He clearly wanted to tell me something. He wanted to get something off his chest. "Ed, I've got some not great news."

"Okay, I'm sure it's no big deal, Mark, just tell me."

"Look, you need more experience," Mark explained. "You know, you haven't coached in college at all. And because of that, I'm sorry, man, but it's just too hard of a sell to get the powers that be at NC State to hire you. Again, I'm really sorry."

Say what? I was devastated. And I was shocked, too—and I think I had every right to be. Look, Mark already knew my experience long before he told me he was going to hire me. My lack of experience wasn't some new information or a revelation. Nothing had changed from when he called me in 2011 to when he met with me in 2012—except that I was further on my way to finishing my college degree so that I could be hired as a college coach. I found the reason he gave to be disingenuous at best and a lie at worst. It was obvious that hiring me was beyond his control and that other factors were at play.

I just told Mark, "Okay, thanks, I'll keep in touch." And I flew back home.

And on the flight home to Vegas I started to connect the dots. I don't know. Maybe Mark wanted to hire me but there was something in my background that was going to be a problem and that he didn't want to mention to my face. If so, I knew what it was: my case against the NCAA. And it was a case that had grown stronger between 2011 and 2012. That's mainly because in May 2011 Judge Wilken refused to dismiss the lawsuit, as the NCAA had thought would happen. Her decision meant that a trial was on the way. Maybe Mark had gotten word from the NCAA that he couldn't bring me on, so he came up with the "need more experience" reason, fake as it was. When I got home, Rosa had the same reaction: this was payback for my taking on the system.

I guess if you speak up against city hall, it really will bite you.

I would learn that lesson again a couple of months later when I called Lorenzo Romar, another former UCLA assistant coach from our championship team, for advice on how to break into coaching.

See, even after my experience with NC State, I still wanted to coach—I had the bug in me. Lorenzo, who at the time was the University of Washington head coach, seemed like the right guy to call. He had periodically told me that I should call him when I was ready to begin my coaching career. Lorenzo also had a long and successful career that received a big boost by our winning the title in 1995. Pepperdine would hire him as head coach the following year. Then St. Louis University and then Washington would hire Lorenzo. He was on the fast track.

When I called Lorenzo he seemed really excited to hear from me. We talked about the life of a coach, and how it's a full-time commitment. Lorenzo detailed just how demanding of a job it can be and how much time I'd need to spend away from my family. To some extent I felt like he was trying to discourage me from pursuing a coaching career. But at the same time, I empha-sized to him how much I wanted a coaching job. I also bluntly told him that I wanted to be on his staff. In fact, I half-kidding-ly said, "Please make up a job if you need to," so that I could become one of his assistant coaches.

Lorenzo then invited me to see him in Washington. He said I would stay at his house and he'd show me around campus. He also talked about meetings with his staff and others in the Huskies athletic department. His school arranged and paid for all of my travel.

I was a little unclear on Lorenzo's message. On one hand, he didn't say that I would be interviewing for a coaching job or that he had a job waiting for me. And in fairness to him, he never mentioned that there was a job opening or that he expected to fill a position. But Lorenzo knew that I really wanted a job on his staff and that I wanted to land my first college coaching gig. Also, the school was paying for my trip—this clearly wasn't a social visit—and the agenda for the trip sure seemed like a job interview. So I was confused, but I accepted Lorenzo's invitation in the hope that it would lead to a job.

Soon thereafter, I packed my bags and flew to Washington. When I met up with Lorenzo, he introduced me to Brad Jackson, a former head coach at Western Washington University whom Lorenzo had just hired as an assistant coach. Jackson, I was then told, had replaced assistant coach Paul Fortier, who had recently joined Cal Poly as an assistant coach. This was all news to me. I didn't know Fortier had left UW or that Jackson was hired to replace him. I then realized that there was no job opening.

Still, Lorenzo and I spoke at length about coaching and at least the concept of my becoming part of UW basketball. We had an in-depth and very positive discussion—that is, until I brought up my lawsuit against the NCAA. I knew I had to say something about it. After all, I had just gotten burned from the TV commentator gig and from the NC State situation. I didn't want that to happen again. It was way too frustrating for my family and me to have to relive it a third time. "I'm not trying to sneak anything by you, coach. I want you to know everything about me and what I'm a part of. And I want to make sure we're on the same page here." I then detailed everything, from watching a boy play a sixty-dollar Xbox video game that had me in it to the day we filed the lawsuit.

To my surprise, Lorenzo responded that he didn't know anything about the case. In my head, I thought, *Wow, how does he not know?* It had been on ESPN and PBS and all over the internet. I knew he was wrapped up in his job and all, but other college coaches knew about the case. They always brought it up when I spoke with them. If Lorenzo had known about my lawsuit would he even have invited me up? I doubt it.

"Ed, I'm not worried about this at all." Verbally, Lorenzo acted like it was no big deal. "Just let me do some research and talk to my AD. Everything's cool, though." While his words were reassuring, Lorenzo's demeanor changed pretty dramatically. I could see his enthusiasm for me fade really fast. He told me that he was tired and wanted to call it a night.

The next day Lorenzo drove me to the airport. He was pretty silent on the drive. At some point I just came out and said it. "Coach, what's up—what do you think?"

"Ed, I'm sorry, man, but you really need more experience."

More experience? Lorenzo was aware of my résumé before I flew out there. What changed, I wondered? Didn't take me long to put two and two together: the program didn't want me after I mentioned the lawsuit.

I'm not angry with my basketball brothers who might've started my coaching career, just a bit frustrated. I know that taking a chance on me would have meant taking a chance on the guy who was suing the NCAA, the organization to which their schools belonged.

I get it. It's complicated.

Still, these people knew me well. They knew my character and dedication. They knew the deep basketball knowledge I could offer. They knew the ability I have to recruit top high school talent. And, frankly, they knew I had played a pretty big role in their careers.

• • •

I think Judge Wilken would have approved had she been judging me for a job. She was like Superman; she could see through anything. She learned about college sports from a completely unbiased perspective, without letting anyone or anything distort the reality of her perception.

Indeed, Judge Wilken demanded facts and then more facts. She left no stone unturned. I had never been around someone so inquisitive, such a true learner in every sense of the word. And I'm sure that, like Rosa, by the end of the trial Judge Wilken was able to name off a full list of college conferences, teams and even coaches. It was a beautiful thing to see.

There was, however, one awkward moment for me with Judge Wilken, and I thought for a second I might have ruined the case for us.

By the second to last day of the trial, Thursday, June 26, I figured I had a pretty good mental impression of Judge Wilken. After all, when you watch the same people every day for three weeks straight, you're kind of like an artist taking in the scene. You begin to see the fine details of a person and you can easily see them if you close your eyes.

So, I knew what Judge Wilken looked like. She had salt-

and-pepper curly hair right at her shoulders. She wasn't very tall—at least she didn't look it while sitting behind the bench. Nonetheless, I had only seen Judge Wilken in her judge's robe. I didn't know what she looked like in regular clothing.

Well, I arrived at the courthouse very early that Thursday. I had had trouble sleeping the night before. I felt a lot of nervous tension. I knew the trial was almost over and it was starting to hit me.

While waiting for the courtroom to open I decided to go to the bathroom, which was down a hallway and around a corner. When I got there I'm pretty sure about half of the lawyers were there too—it must have been end-of-trial anxiety!

Anyway, after I left the bathroom, I was walking back around the hallway corner and I saw this lady with her hands completely full while trying to open the door. She was dressed in business attire. Maybe she was a lawyer or a clerk. She was maybe five foot four and had gray hair.

My mom raised me to open doors for women and my instinct kicked in: go open the door for this woman. So I did just that, and came from behind her to open the door. I still hadn't seen her face. Then we turned to each other, and it was Judge Wilken! She realized who I was too. She had that "oh, no" look on her face and I'm sure I had it too. No smiles. Total awkwardness. In fact, she completely avoided making eye contact. She probably didn't need to see my face to realize that the black man standing next to her, a man who was a foot and a half taller than her, was the plaintiff in her trial. She did, however, quietly say, "Thank you," and then hustled into the room.

Damn, I thought. Had I just tampered in the trial? Did I break a law? I had watched enough episodes of *Law and Order* to know that I shouldn't be talking to the judge during recess. It was a scary moment for me. Now I was feeling more nervous walking back into the courtroom than I had felt before I went to the bathroom. I wished I had just held it in!

When I got back to the courtroom I told Michael Hausfeld about what happened. He laughed and said not to worry about it. I felt a lot better after hearing that. And for the short remainder of the trial, I wouldn't be opening doors for anyone!

CHAPTER 10

HOOPS ECONOMICS

THERE WERE QUITE A FEW PEOPLE FROM THE TRIAL WHO LEFT their mark on me. Among them were the economists who testified. While no doubt brilliant, they were at times really hard to follow. They spoke their own language, and I didn't see a translator in the room.

But two economists—Berkeley professor Daniel Rubinfeld, who testified for the NCAA, and Stanford professor Roger Noll, who testified for us—caught my careful attention. They commented on topics with which I was quite familiar.

Look, I understand that professional athletes are stereotyped as not always seeming particularly sophisticated or well spoken, but they do get economics. Trust me. It's thrust on them on during their athletic lives.

I know this from my own life.

• • •

Let me take you back in time to 1995. As you know, I had refused to let a failed dunk ruin my life as a UCLA basketball player. But that chapter of life would come to a natural end when I entered the NBA draft. I didn't graduate from UCLA at the time, as I was still a semester short on coursework. I'd complete those credits a dozen years later. In the meantime, I had a pro basketball career to pursue.

And it was a career that I was very excited about. Although the NBA draft is an inexact science, I had received feedback from friends and people in the industry that I would be a lottery pick. To be chosen by one of the fourteen teams that, by virtue of not making the NBA playoffs, received one of the first fourteen picks in the NBA draft would be a real honor.

The NBA, like other pro leagues, rewards "bad" teams by giving them first dibs on the best amateur players. And if those players don't like the team that drafts them, their only option is to hold out and not report—and thus not get paid or play in the NBA—and hope they get traded to another team.

At first glance it seems a strange way of doing things. We don't say that the valedictorian of Harvard Medical School can be drafted by the worst hospital in the country and that he or she must work at that hospital if they want to practice medicine in the United States. And we don't send the country's top journalism student to a newspaper that's about to go out of business. But we basically do that in sports. The logic is that it helps the league in the long run if the weakest teams have a chance to become competitive.

Being a lottery pick also has financial implications. The earlier you are drafted, the more money you'll be able to sign for. I remembered what happened the prior year. In 1994 Purdue forward Glenn Robinson, the first player picked in that year's draft, signed a contract with the Milwaukee Bucks worth $68 million. I knew there was a chance I could be one of the first few players picked in the 1995 NBA draft. That didn't mean I'd also get $68 million, but I had reason to think I'd be getting a lot of money. Based on conversations I'd had with coaches, I was confident that I wouldn't fall past the tenth pick.

Little did I know, however, that 1995 would become the first year that the NBA would institute a "rookie wage scale," which greatly lowered the value of contracts for rookie players.

Not good timing for me.

And, in truth, there were a lot of things that I didn't know back then that I would have to learn only through experience. Much of it was about the business of sports, but more than anything else, I could have used a crash course on personal finance and financial literacy. Just the basics would have been fine. You see, when you're a college athlete who's making the transition into professional sports, you're probably not well equipped to make that jump.

There's a good chance, for instance, that you've never held a paying job. And you probably have never opened or balanced a checking account. Probably haven't wired money or negotiated a car deal, either. Bought a house and signed a mortgage? Prepared federal and state income taxes? Forget about it. It's all Greek to you.

Yet, over a period of weeks, you're expected to negotiate multimillion-dollar employment and endorsement contracts. To help you, you're supposed to interview potential agents and numerous financial advisors. They promise you that their expertise will, for a healthy price or commission, make you more money. No one, though, tells you what questions to ask those agents and advisors during interviews. Your parents probably don't know what to ask, either. And if you don't know any better, you might end up trusting anything and everything you're told.

Plus, the people you interview all start to sound pretty similar after a while. They all claim to be "insiders," and that they know exactly what you need to do to become Rookie of the Year and an All-Star. Most of them give off that air of self-importance, too. They try to be flashy and make you think they're well connected—it's amazing how many people claim to know Michael Jordan! After meeting with them, you honestly don't know how to distinguish one from the other, other than gut feeling.

Even if all goes well and you hire a great agent who negotiates lucrative contracts on your behalf, you're then expected to manage millions of dollars. Your financial advisor can help, to some degree. But, look, a full-time student basketball player just wasn't given even basic training in these things. Soon I would be receiving a check every two weeks that was worth about $25,000 after taxes.

The transition is jarring.

At the same time, more people than ever watch you play your sport and they expect you to immediately produce. And you're playing against players who are bigger, stronger, faster, and flat-out better than anyone you've ever encountered.

I don't know any human being who is well equipped to make this jump. A soon-to-be NBA player's life up until to that point in time is about two things: playing basketball and trying to get better at playing basketball. This isn't necessarily a bad thing—it helps us become world-class players—but as we age we realize that the people around us know way more than we do about the way the world works.

Sometimes you feel like Tom Hanks in the movie *Big*. You look like an adult. You sound like an adult. But there are parts of you that aren't adult.

I played basketball, almost every day and year-round, from

when I was twelve to when I retired from the game at thirty-two. During high school and college, when a lot of my friends would get summer jobs or intern at big businesses and government offices, I'd be playing ball on traveling teams and in tournaments. It was all hoops. That was true during winter breaks, too, when I'd play every day other than Christmas. Actually, some years I'd play on Christmas, too. There was no period of the year when I didn't play basketball. It never stopped.

My classmates, through summer jobs or semesters abroad, would pick up life lessons and practical tips that I never received. I didn't really get those until I played in the NBA and then lived and played in Europe as a twenty-something-year-old husband and father of three.

And it wasn't that my parents or friends withheld information or anything like that. It was that I was usually around coaches and other players. Their lives had led them to a similarly limited view of the world. When no one knows better, no one knows better.

And I don't want to undervalue the role of coaches in developing athletes as human beings. It's not just sports skills that coaches teach. It's also life skills, like the importance of commitment and hard work. And it's realizing that making excuses isn't a defense. And valuing that punctuality matters—it's better to be thirty minutes early for practice than one minute late, because if you're a minute late then you'll be sitting out or running laps.

The basketball lifestyle shaped my entire world around me, including in college. While our classmates went on dates to restaurants and movie theaters, Rosa and I spent a lot of time in the not-so-romantic Pauley Pavilion. This is where the basketball team played at UCLA. She would sit there in the stands, hours at a time, reading books from her courses. From time to time she would look up and watch me shoot free throw after free throw and jump shot after jump shot. I always appreciated her being there. She did all this while she balanced owning and helping to manage a clothing and accessories boutique. I don't know how she did it all. And yet despite taking a full-time course load and running a business, she would tell me that I worked more than she did. I just wasn't paid for my work.

And the life of nonstop sports doesn't just affect the athlete. In a lot of ways, the schedule takes over the lives of family members, too. Take a holiday like Thanksgiving. Families normally get together on Thanksgiving. A lot of families would say it's not a real family holiday if a son or daughter is missing. But for basketball players, Thanksgiving often means tournaments, road trips, and time away from family. In college I lived a short drive from the homes of my parents and Rosa's folks, yet I didn't spend Thanksgiving with them because of basketball commitments. One year we had a road trip and spent Thanksgiving in Buffalo, New York. Coach Harrick's wife, Sally, played the role of our surrogate mom and cooked us a delicious meal.

Your coach isn't just your coach. In a lot of ways he's the head of your family and your team becomes your social life. Who you hang out with, who you date—everything runs through the team.

You never question this state of affairs while it plays out. It's just taken as a given. You don't know any better. If your family wants to spend time with you on holidays, they need to travel with you for games. But if they aren't there, that's okay, too. Not only does no one complain but no one even thinks about complaining.

Depending on your parents' jobs and their available resources, they may not always be able to travel with you. Flights and hotels can be expensive. The same is true for eating out at restaurants and renting a car. Time off from work isn't always possible.

So when I talk about using the law and economics to make the college experience a normal one for college athletes, I'm talking about these types of experiences. Use money generated from the licensing of names, images, and likenesses to help out families of players so traveling isn't so costly. Make being a parent of a college athlete while he or she is on the road possible for them, too. Don't leave them out of the discussion.

In addition to the draft lottery system and the shock of facing financial management, I received another crash course in economics three days after the NBA draft. On July 1, 1995, the NBA locked out all NBA players—rookies included—due to a disagreement with the players' association over a new collective bargaining agreement. The reason for the lockout was the same reason for any labor dispute in pro sports: the owners and players couldn't decide on how to divide up billions of dollars. It was notable, though, because it was the first time in NBA history the league had locked out its players.

You might say it wasn't the ideal time to enter the NBA.

The lockout meant that the Nets couldn't sign me to a contract. In fact, they couldn't have any contact with me. No phone calls. No faxes. No emails, though they were new back then. That's how lockouts work: it's a complete separation between the team and player. I felt like I had been an NBA player for three days and then my team had gone AWOL.

This meant I wouldn't be paid any salary. And I couldn't work out with the team and practice. I wouldn't get to know the coaching staff and my teammates until this lockout was over. I also really didn't know what was going on with the labor negotiations, since I was a rookie of all of three days and had little access to information. My only source of info was Arn Tellem, who, as an agent, wasn't in the bargaining sessions and could only share what he knew.

It was a disruptive way to start my NBA career, to say the least.

By September the owners and players had worked out a new collective bargaining agreement. The good news was that no regular season games were lost. The bad news: in order to strike a deal and keep veteran players' salaries high, the union essentially traded away the financial interests of rookie players.

They did so by agreeing to a rookie wage scale, which owners wanted in light of Glenn Robinson's huge contract from the year before. The scale dictated that rookie players can only sign three-year contracts and for much less money than previous seasons' rookies obtained. Let me show you how much it impacted salaries. Whereas Robinson, the first player selected in the 1994 NBA draft, signed a ten-year deal worth $68 million, Joe Smith, the player selected first in the 1995 NBA draft, signed a three-year deal worth $8.5 million. The difference all had to do with the wage scale.

It was frustrating that my fellow rookies and I had virtually no influence over the negotiations. I get that veteran players do the negotiating, but we were NBA players for only three days when the lockout commenced. Talk about having no say over what happens.

In early October I signed a three-year contract with the Nets worth $3.9 million. It was a lot of money, to be sure, but also less guaranteed money than the $20 million Eric Montross had received from the Boston Celtics in the previous year when he, like me, was drafted ninth overall. I remember doing a compare-and-contrast between my contract and that of Montross and saying to myself, *Oh my God. If they had just waited one more year to do a new collective bargaining agreement…*

Still, I had made it and I would be set financially. It's hard to complain about earning nearly $4 million in any occupation.

And I remember getting my first NBA paycheck. I'm not the type of person to do anything crazy with new money, but I decided to do something special this one time: I combined my NBA paycheck with signing-bonus checks from my Nike endorsement deal. I then bought my brother and myself matching Ford SUVs.

At the O'Bannon Foundation Summer Basketball Camp. My father, Charles, and me.

I got him a white one and I took a black one. The whole experience was a surprise to him, too. My dad and I had picked up Charles and we drove over to a local dealership in LA. Dad and I told Charles we wanted his advice on what I should buy and he said sure, whatever.

After we picked a car to buy, I told the car salesman, "Make that two." Charles was stunned. "Are you serious?"

"I am."

I felt awesome. It was a great day for the O'Bannon family.

I did some other spending, too. I helped my parents pay some bills, and Rosa and I bought a condo in Manhattan Beach. But for the most part I approached my NBA salary in a conservative and cautious way. I was a father and had a family to take care of. People I loved depended on me. So, no, I didn't buy a Lamborghini or some of the other crazy things that rookie players do. *Keep it simple* has always been my mantra.

• • •

When the economists testified in my trial, I wasn't as naïve or ignorant as I think some people might have assumed.

Let me take the testimony of Berkeley professor Daniel Rubinfeld first. He seemed like a nice enough fellow, but he got the NCAA into a bit of a bind when it was revealed that he had previously called the NCAA a "cartel" in one of his books.

Hmm. "Cartel."

When I think of cartels, here's what comes to mind: Pablo Escobar. OPEC. You know, bad things! Certainly not the kind of company you want to keep if you are the NCAA. And there's a reason why you never hear of "good cartels," at least not until my trial.

Rubinfeld explained why in his 2013 book *Microeconomics*. In it, he wrote that the NCAA was a cartel because of the NCAA's "persistently high levels of profits" that were "inconsistent with competition."

Now, like I mentioned, I'm no economist and I don't pretend to be. But after nearly a decade of litigation against the NCAA, I've learned quite a bit about the basics of a cartel. It's an agreement among competitors to act as one. By doing so, the cartel limits competition and manipulates prices. The losers of the NCAA cartel are college sports consumers, who pay more, and college athletes, who don't get paid.

The NCAA easily meets the definition of a cartel, and particularly in relation to what we were arguing. There was no doubt that the NCAA acted on behalf of competing schools and conferences to set the value of players' names, images, and likenesses at zero dollars. That way, the NCAA and its members kept the money that should have gone to players.

The thing is, schools and conferences not only agreed to not compete with one another, but because they realized that their natural inclination was to compete—they are, after all, competing for all sorts of things—they also agreed to being monitored by the NCAA for purposes of compliance. Heck, they even agreed to being punished by the NCAA if any of them tried to raise the value of a player's name, image, and likeness rights from zero dollars to something higher.

In other words, if you took a college out of the NCAA, it would not only have no problem paying student athletes but that college would actually *want* to pay them as a recruiting tool. We know this because colleges compete with each other all the time to recruit the best high school students. Those schools offer high school academic stars various enticements in the form of scholarships, access to resources, internships, fellowships—you name it. They do so because they are acting according to their true nature: competitors.

Rubinfeld's own published words supported this point. Needless to say, I was very surprised that the NCAA would hire an economist whose own writings advanced our argument.

Now, Rubinfeld tried to talk himself out of the ditch. He described the NCAA as an innocent joint venture that, in ways that he had never made clear, advanced higher education. It was almost like he was trying to complicate the topic as a way of distracting Judge Wilken from what he had actually written. It didn't work. The same goes for attempts by Greg Curtner to reframe the cartel topic. I chuckled when he told Judge Wilken that the NCAA was a "cartel that does good things." Whatever that is!

Our economist, Roger Noll, also left an impression on me. He is an older fellow, with white hair and glasses. If at this very moment you imagined an economist lecturing a class, someone who looks kind of like Noll might come to mind. He played the part.

Noll also was really persuasive. First off, he completely debunked the depiction of the NCAA as a "cartel that does good things." As Noll explained, cartels "prevent members from self-interest." He stressed that if not for NCAA rules and the threat of NCAA penalties, schools would gladly compensate athletes for, among other things, the use of their names, images, and likenesses. Noll mentioned how the Power Five conferences (the Atlantic Coast Conference, Big Ten, Big 12, Pac-12, and the Southeastern Conference) would like to see amateurism rules made less severe because those conferences are disadvantaged by not being able to better compensate student athletes. Schools only care about "amateurism" to the extent that it's a requirement for membership in the cartel.

Noll also showed that he had done his homework. He cited a study proving that salaries of college coaches had risen by 512 percent since 1985. During that same time period college presidents' salaries had climbed only 108 percent. Noll had similar numbers on how universities kept building bigger and better stadiums and more advanced and sophisticated athletic facilities. His point was clear: colleges have been earning huge money from sports but, because of amateurism, they can only spend it on things surrounding the athletes, not on the athletes themselves.

Noll really captured what drove the lawsuit: college sports generate massive amounts of revenue, and universities are in an arms race with each other to generate even more revenue. Yet through the NCAA, those same universities agree not to compete on the players who generate that revenue. That's the crux of the situation. And it was one Judge Wilken clearly detected and thought needed to change.

CHAPTER 11

CLOSURE

THE TRIAL WOULD END ON FRIDAY, JUNE 27. THREE WEEKS doesn't sound like a long time, but three weeks of a *trial* sure feels like three months.

I realize that I didn't have to be at the trial once I was done testifying. But there was no way I was going to miss it. Still, court can get repetitive and tiring. More than two dozen witnesses had testified. Some of the witnesses made the same basic arguments as other witnesses and answered the same basic set of questions, often with similar responses.

After the long haul, I wanted a firm decision from Judge Wilken that last day, too. Win or lose, I wanted to fly back to Vegas with Rosa and have closure to this chapter of my life.

That feeling brought me back to the day I decided to end my

basketball career. It was during the summer of 2004, when I was in Oregon to try out to play in a Japanese league.

• • •

I was thirty-two years old and had played eleven seasons in the NBA and abroad. I had also undergone multiple knee surgeries and accompanying rehabs. To be honest, I was tired of moving from country to country every year. My family had followed me everywhere but had, understandably, gotten sick of a nomadic existence. We bought a house in Carson, right next to Los Angeles, and Rosa had moved into it with the kids. She was ready for us to settle down and provide stability for our children.

So there I was at the University of Oregon for a tryout with the Japan Basketball League. My knees were shot and my heart was no longer in it. I hate to admit it, but I was going through the motions in front of those Japanese coaches. And halfway through the tryout I politely told the Japanese head coach that this wasn't for me. I literally walked off the court. I was done. I hadn't completely lost the love for the game that had, to that point, largely defined my life, but I had lost the desire to keep fighting for roster spots.

I called Rosa and told her I was coming home, for good. I even left my sneakers in the dormitory. I didn't need them anymore.

I knew my basketball career was over, but I didn't know what to do next. I had no postbasketball career plan.

Rosa suggested, and gradually pushed, for us to move to Las Vegas—a place we'd always loved vacationing in but also met a list of conditions that included good schools, safe neighborhoods, and locations where our kids could play sports against top athletes. Rosa knew it was a good place to start fresh.

Initially I hated the idea. I was an LA kid and I was finally home. I didn't want to relocate yet again. But the idea grew on me. Housing prices were so much cheaper in Vegas than in LA and we bought ourselves a great home for the kids. And we bought a second home there, too, all for less than the price of one house in LA.

While Rosa worked full-time with disadvantaged children *and* pursued a master's degree in educational counseling *and* spent hours each night on her homework and with our children on their homework, I spent a lot of time on the couch, watching TV. I didn't know what I wanted to do for a career. The one thing I was good at had faded with age and injury. I felt like I didn't have much to offer. And I was tired and needed a break. Nobody could tell me when the break should end.

Eventually, Rosa gave me The Talk.

She had picked up the kids at school on her way back from work. It was about 5:30 p.m. when she arrived, and her day had begun at 5 a.m. With her own homework still to do and helping the kids with theirs, her day probably wouldn't be over until close to midnight. Meanwhile, I lay there on the couch in our living room, feeling kind of down, watching TV but not really focused on what I was watching. Zoned out.

Rosa walked into our living room. I could see the fury in her face. And every bit of it was deserved. Between work, school, and our kids, she was working a twenty-hour day. And here I was watching TV and feeling sorry for myself. "You know, marriage is a partnership!" Rosa screamed at me. "I'm not the only one working in this relationship. You need to work. Our savings aren't going to last forever."

I didn't say anything at that point. I mean, I didn't really have a defense. What was I going to say? She was speaking the truth.

And she continued.

"You need to get off the couch and find something to do. You need a purpose, Ed. *You're better than this!*"

It was the wake-up call I needed. I had fallen into a spiral that a lot of athletes fall into when their careers end. Your whole life up until that point has been on a schedule and you never needed much self-direction in that regard. You always knew what you had to do: work as hard as you can at your game. You never needed a résumé or a list of references. You didn't need to think about careers and professional advancement. It was just: play sports.

So I got up off the couch and picked myself up by my boot-straps, swallowed my pride, and started looking for jobs. I was no longer Ed O'Bannon the basketball player. I was Ed O'Bannon the job hunter.

I hadn't yet completed my degree at UCLA—I would eight years later—so jobs requiring a college degree were not in the cards. But I saw an ad for a sales and leasing consultant at Findlay Toyota. It was right near my house. I called and they said to come on in for an interview.

Now, I'm not a car guy. I had never worked on cars and I only knew the basics that people in general know. I was also up-front about that in my interview. There's no point lying or exaggerating—I wanted to work at a place where I would succeed.

Then I met Findlay's general manager, Rich Abajian, in the interview. He told me he wasn't a car guy either and that it's all about being a people person, and he could tell I was one. He said it's about relationships and treating others how you want to be treated. "You don't necessarily sell a car," Rich told me. "You help someone purchase one."

Rich basically outlined how to act if you want to act like the opposite of the NCAA!

I'm not surprised Rich got it. He was, like me, a former jock. He had played college football at the University of Nevada, Reno, and later coached the secondary in UNLV's football program. He knew what it was all about. Like other athletes, he valued the things I valued—loyalty, responsibility, and meeting clear expectations. And he also understood the transition I was making. Rich was the ideal person for me to meet at that point in my life. And until he passed away in 2016, Rich was always there to help me.

Rich offered me the job on the spot and I took it. I ended up doing really well and was promoted every year. I approached selling cars with the understanding that there are two places people hate to be at: car lots and the dentist's office. And most of the people looking to buy a car don't want to deal with that annoying car guy. They don't want fast-talking, salesperson lingo. They just want to know a little about the car and then decide if they want it. I don't pressure anyone.

And as my car career took off, college sports became a distant memory. Other than during March, when people would call me to talk about March Madness, I didn't spend time thinking about basketball. I didn't watch many games. I basically closed the book on that part of my life. I hadn't forgotten about what had happened with the NCAA. But I knew that there was nothing I could do about it.

All of that would, of course, change in April 2009 when I watched Spencer control Ed O'Bannon the video game avatar. But the larger point is that I'm used to the sports model. A game is played and a winner emerges at the end of the game. And both sides accept the outcome and then go home. When you retire, you retire and move on to the next chapter in life.

But that's not how the law works.

• • •

Michael Hausfeld and the other lawyers cautioned that it would likely be months before Judge Wilken decided. They explained that she would take time to review what she had heard in the trial and read over legal filings. Then she would take several weeks to draft an opinion. Then, as Michael warned, "there would be appeals" that possibly could take years.

If nothing else, law is deliberate. You might call it slow, but *deliberate* is probably the better word since the issues at stake are important and complex. They deserve serious thought and that takes time.

Closing arguments were a chance to hear each side's best last pitch to Judge Wilken. It reminded me of a college coach laying it all on the line in recruiting a high school player. The coach is going to make his or her most persuasive argument to convince the player and his or her family that this particular college is the right one to pick.

Judge Wilken, though, isn't some seventeen-year-old kid. Nor is she a well-intentioned but naïve parent. She is an extremely bright legal mind who wouldn't fall for any lawyerly head-fakes.

And Judge Wilken asked the lawyers questions during their closing arguments, which I later learned is uncommon during trials. Usually the lawyers talk and sit down. But my case was anything but usual, so I think it was fitting that we did things a little differently.

Glenn Pomerantz delivered the NCAA's closing case. Although I was no fan of his, I thought he spoke with conviction and eloquence. The man is a talented attorney, no doubt. He tried to reframe the case so that it worked for the NCAA's legal theories. The effort was there. So too was the passion.

The result? Not so much.

Pomerantz's core point was that whether amateurism rules are unfair wasn't for Judge Wilken to decide. Instead, he insisted, she should only consider whether consumers are hurt by those rules. He argued this point by claiming that consumers, not athletes or students, are the primary focus of antitrust law. With that in mind, Pomerantz asserted that amateurism has led to numerous TV broadcasts of college games and the overall popularity of college sports.

This was not a crazy point. In fact, it wasn't wrong. Many college sports fans like the idea of college sports being separate from pro sports. I'm one of them, actually.

But as Judge Wilken later wrote, this defense didn't address our arguments. We weren't trying to turn college sports into pro sports. We were trying to protect the legal rights of college players and former players from having their identities commercially exploited by the NCAA and its business partners.

Pomerantz's other contentions fell on deaf ears. He warned that schools would drop sports programs if I won. I don't think anyone was buying that fantasy anymore. The cloak on the NCAA's bogeyman had been lifted. If the trial had taken place in 1994 or 2004 Pomerantz might have enjoyed some traction with that argument. But in 2014? No way.

Pomerantz also rehashed NCAA-sponsored research that amateurism somehow helps to direct college athletes to focus on academics. We had thoroughly rebuked that theory during the trial. Just because you say it over and over again doesn't make it true.

Likewise, fears that opportunistic agents would soon be flooding college campuses to snatch up college athletes didn't sway Judge Wilken. As we talked about during the trial, if we won, college athletes would not negotiate with individual agents representing them. Instead, they would use a group license.

Our original plan was that a trade association would offer to represent any and all Division I college athletes. On their behalf, the trade association would negotiate licenses with the NCAA, conferences, and individual colleges for the right to use those players' names, images, and likenesses. As for former players, the expectation was that Kenneth Feinberg—the arbitrator who was placed in charge of victim funds for the September 11th terrorist attack and the Boston Marathon bombings—would lead the "Former College Athletes Association," or FCAA, to negotiate for ex-players like me. This way, former players would have a voice when they appear in video games, classic broadcasts, and trading cards.

So, no, college athletes wouldn't be distracted from studies if I won. Just the opposite, actually—they would know their rights are being protected, not only while they are in school but for years afterward. If anything, the success of our case would help college athletes focus better on school and sports.

Judge Wilken also seemed skeptical of Pomerantz's appealing to history as a way of justifying the present. He went on and on about how in the 124-year history of federal antitrust law, no court has ever ruled on a case involving athletes' name, image, and likeness rights and federal antitrust law. Pomerantz harped on college athletes not being consumers of the NCAA, and so no consumers were being hurt by NCAA rules.

She saw through this logic. First, consumers may be hurt by NCAA rules since they limit competition for athletes' identity rights. Second, Pomerantz was ignoring that antitrust law doesn't look kindly upon anticompetitive practices. We weren't even seeking pay for our identity rights. We simply wanted the right to negotiate pay, and that's all. Third, as Judge Wilken highlighted, my case raised novel issues that no court had previously examined. And just because the NCAA's system has been in place for decades doesn't mean it ought to have.

Then the stage turned to my guys, Michael Hausfeld and Bill Isaacson, to make my final case to Judge Wilken. As I watched Michael and Bill stand and deliver a tour de force argument, I thought, *This is like watching the Michael Jordan and Scottie Pippen of lawyers work their magic.* They were first-rate, from start to finish. They were truly champions.

And they began with the obvious: I attended UCLA to play basketball. It's why the coaching staff recruited me. It's why the dean of admissions accepted me. It's why the dean for financial aid waived my tuition and housing fees. This point undercut the NCAA's assertion that its system of amateurism was designed to safeguard the academic experience for student-athletes.

Amateurism has never been about academics, education, or learning. Amateurism is really about two things. First, it creates and imposes rules to ensure that the wealth generated by college sports is only shared among some and only shared in certain ways. And second, it supplies lawmakers, media, and fans with a work of fiction—the romanticized narrative of the college athlete as an innocent amateur uncorrupted by professional sports and its business partners. A lot of people *want* to believe in that fiction because it sounds like *Hoosiers* or *Rudy*. Heck, I want to believe in it. But it isn't true, at all.

As Michael and Bill stressed in their closing argument, my own experience at UCLA proved there was no "balance" between academics and athletics. They also reminded Judge Wilken that everyone who is on the inside—the NCAA, school officials, coaches, broadcast partners, and, yes, the players—knows that so-called balance couldn't be further from the truth.

Look, not one of my teammates stuck to under twenty hours per week on sports, as is supposedly required by the NCAA. And why would they? *They were there to play sports!* Plus, even if they wanted to focus on schoolwork and bench their sports commitments, they would have risked losing their spot on the team and thus losing their scholarship and jeopardizing their ability to pay tuition. If anything, the NCAA's system of amateurism was designed to push student-athletes *away* from academics. Once you start to unravel the NCAA's talking points, you uncover a long list of contradictions and discrepancies.

Michael and Bill weren't done in making their last pitch to

Judge Wilken. They then ridiculed all the warnings we heard from various NCAA witnesses during the trial that schools were about to leave Division I if I won the case. Think about it. Schools that generate untold millions of dollars would suddenly seek to leave Division I if players were eligible to receive what they were owed under the law? That's the best line of reasoning the NCAA has to offer? Really?

Schools do everything they can to join Division I, which, after all, is what is meant by "big-time college sports." Membership in Division I means more money, more exposure, and more attention for your school. I mean no disrespect to Division II and Division III. They have their place in college sports and in higher education. For some colleges that prioritize academics and that prefer to schedule games locally so they don't interfere with student-athletes' studies, Division II and Division III are much better fits than Division I. But they are also very different from Division I. Division III doesn't allow any athletic scholarships, and while Division II permits partial athletic scholarships, those schools tend to have higher graduation rates than Division I schools and lower student-to-teacher ratios.

What matters here is that my case didn't alter the equation of whether it makes sense for a college to want to be in Division I, Division II, or Division III.

Along those lines, notice that my case didn't scare away Abilene Christian University, Grand Canyon University, the University of the Incarnate Word, or the University of Massachusetts Lowell from jumping through every hoop and dotting every *i* to move up from Division II to Division I in 2013. Nor did my victory in 2014 cause them to change their mind and not become full Division I members in 2017. It also hasn't deterred either California Baptist University or the University of North Alabama from making the jump to Division I in 2018.

Michael and Bill also took aim at the NCAA's fearmongering that college athletes compensated for the commercial use of their names, images, and likenesses would alienate fans. NCAA witnesses had insisted that, from a fan's point of view, my victory would degrade NCAA college hoops into a lesser version of the NBA's Developmental League, now known as the G-League. As an example, Mark Lewis, the NCAA's executive vice president overseeing championship events, had testified that March Madness would take a serious financial hit if I won. "I don't think," Lewis told Judge Wilken, "people would be as interested to watch a tournament with professionals playing amateurs."

Lewis also suggested that any form of "paying" college athletes would undermine what college fans love most: the David and Goliath narrative, where a school comes out of nowhere in the tournament and upsets bigger-name schools. A recent example would be the fifth-seed Butler University Bulldogs nearly toppling the first-seed Duke University Blue Devils in the 2010 National Championship Game.

Look, I loved watching Butler play in the 2010 tournament. The championship game against Duke, where Butler lost by just two points, was an all-time classic. Gordon Hayward. Shelvin Mack. Coach Brad Stevens. These guys were for real. They represented the entire Butler community with such class.

But let's say that Hayward and Mack—Butler's best players—had received compensation from the NCAA and CBS for the use of their names, images, and likenesses during the tournament (a tournament, by the way, in which the final game attracted twenty-four million television viewers, the highest number of viewers in ten years). I'm not talking about a paycheck for Hayward and Mack's labor. I'm talking about an amount that reflects the fair share of their identities being used to generate all that TV money.

Would anyone have been any less interested in watching Butler as the underdog?

Would anyone who was going to watch the Butler-Duke championship game not have done so?

Would fans really dismiss Hayward and Mack as "poor man's NBA D Leaguers," whatever that means?

And would those same fans complain, "these guys aren't really students!" and then change the channel?

If none of that sounds especially believable, then you, Judge Wilken, and I are all in agreement.

Bill nailed this point in the closing argument. As he stressed, my case wasn't about turning student-athletes into professional athletes or university employees. This point echoed Roger Noll's earlier testimony when he noted that a student-athlete's ability to pursue a degree wouldn't be harmed by that same student-athlete being eligible to receive fair compensation. And that gets at what our case was really about: not letting schools and the NCAA conspire to commercially exploit the identities of student athletes. That's really it. And the idea that fans would lose their fervor if a federal judge ruled that an illegal conspiracy is, in fact, illegal would be almost laughable if it weren't also so insulting to everyone's intelligence.

Colleges and the NCAA wouldn't lose a dollar if I won. Everyone sitting in that courtroom knew it. And guess what? After I won, revenue for the March Madness tournament has only climbed each year.

I give the NCAA credit: they know how to market a product really well. They understand what appeals to their customers and they know how to craft a narrative. Make no mistake—I know the NCAA employs many talented people. They are anything but incompetent. But just because the NCAA is skilled at marketing the names, images, and likeness of players doesn't mean those players should automatically receive nothing. It's like there's a giant gap in logic that a lot of people accept because it's been that way for many years. "That's just the way it is" isn't a good reason.

And all I've asked is that the people who actually produce the product get to negotiate for a mere slice of the share.

And that was the case. Judge Wilken smiled and thanked everyone. She then dismissed both sides.

I felt so relieved for the trial to be over. As I walked away from our courtroom table for the last time, I looked at Rosa. I knew that we were both thinking the same exact thing: *We really did it. This case. This trial. We did it. And we're still standing proud.*

That wasn't our only shared thought. I know both Rosa and I were also thinking, *We'll soon be boarding a flight back to Vegas and getting back to our regular lives.* A return to normalcy is exactly what we needed.

But before then we had a little bit of celebrating to do.

Once outside of the courtroom, Sathya told me that there would be a congratulatory lunch upstairs in one of the boardrooms.

Rosa and I took the elevator up there and all of my lawyers and the Vaccaros were present—the whole team. Mr. and Mrs. Vaccaro gave me the biggest hugs I can ever recall. They told me how proud they were of me, and I told them I was just as proud of them. This was a war we had all fought in.

We then held hands as a group and thanked each other. It was a beautiful thing. We had done everything that we could over the previous few weeks—really, over the previous six years. It was now in Judge Wilken's hands and we would await her judgment.

I think, health-wise, it was a positive for our entire team for the trial to have ended. The experience was clearly wearing on everyone. The pressure had been building each day and never abated. From the circles and bags under everyone's eyes to the worsening coughs to the raspy voices—I could go on—there had been many sleepless nights.

So you might say it was time for the buzzer to go off and for the game to end. It was time to walk off the floor.

And we did just that. Rosa and I hopped on a flight back home to Nevada. Literally within a day we had resumed our daily routines. I felt great getting back to Findlay and jumping right back into work. It was like I hadn't missed a beat.

• • •

After the trial ended, plenty of people shared their views about my case. A number of current and former athletes emailed or tweeted at me to say thank you for standing up. It didn't matter which sport they played or whether they were men or women. Sometimes it was former basketball players. Other times it was former volleyball or track athletes. To a person, they were supportive. Not one player had anything negative to say. Quite a few former players also told me they viewed the case as about racial justice. They knew that I'm not a civil rights leader. No one is confusing me with Malcolm X or Gandhi. But the thing is, you didn't need to be someone of that stature or courage to recognize a very simple point: the NCAA has made a lot of money off the backs of young black men, and there's something very disconcerting about that. So players embraced our cause and, in doing so, made me feel proud that I had brought the case.

It was a different story for people who hadn't played sports and who wished to contact me about the case. There it was a mixed bag. Some of those folks were, like the athletes, encouraging, but others had less flattering views. I never received any death threats, but I would get the occasional message that wished me harm. Most of the responses, though, looked like these three:

"Why are you doing this?"

"You're just some money-hungry ex-jock!"

"Dude, you're messing up the video games!"

The "why" critique was an easy question to answer. And no, I obviously wasn't "money hungry." If I were, I wouldn't have spent eight years of my life litigating a case where I knew that if I won, I would get the same amount of money as if I lost: zero dollars. In fact, all things considered, I likely lost quite a bit of money on the case. Rosa and I spent some serious funds on travel, and both of us took time away from work—and, remember, I sell cars. So when I'm not at work selling cars, I'm not getting a commission and I'm not getting paid.

But the video game comment was the one that I got the most. To be honest, it kind of caught me off guard since it was so wrong and so ridiculous. Yes, it's true that Electronic Arts stopped publishing college sports games after we filed my lawsuit, but let's think about the facts for a moment.

First off, as the evidence showed, Electronic Arts wanted to pay for the right to use complete player identities. It wanted every college roster and every roster of top teams from the past. It wanted every college player's name. It wanted a license to publish everything about the players and their identities within college hoops. EA didn't care if it had to pay the NCAA, the schools, the players, the former players, or some combination of them for that right.

This isn't surprising at all if you think about it. EA is in the business of making video games. It's not in the business of propping up amateurism. It doesn't care about amateurism. Never has. Never will.

And consider EA's slogan for its sports video games, "It's in the game." EA only wants to publish the most realistic sports games possible. Why is that? Because the most realistic games are the kinds of games that sell the best.

So why aren't there college games with complete players' identities? It's because of the NCAA.

The NCAA told EA that the video game publisher couldn't pay for the complete identity rights of college players. So that stopped EA from obtaining them. If the NCAA had let EA pay us, all of you gamers out there would have your college sports games. So don't blame me. Blame the NCAA for refusing to change its rules in the face of basic common sense, not to mention consumer demand.

Plus, EA reached a settlement with us right before the trial. We have no grievance with them and they have no grievance with us. The settlement called for EA to pay about $40 million to more than twenty-nine thousand current and former players who were part of our class action. Depending on how many games the players appeared in and how closely their likeness was directly copied in the game's avatars, players got checks worth up to $7,200 and on average about $1,200. The checks obviously didn't come from the NCAA, so they didn't "right the wrong" that the NCAA had inflicted on college athletes. I also recognize that a check for five figures didn't make any player rich, but our case—our movement—was never about making anyone rich. It was about fairness and recognition of rights.

And I should add that my lawyers consulted with me about the settlement and asked for my approval. They explained why they believed it made sense. They asked me if it was enough or if we should keep fighting. It was one of those conversations where we all agreed that two plus two equals four but they said we could wait it out and try to make it equal five. I said, no, two plus two equals four. And so we struck a deal with EA and that removed EA from the case.

EA settled in part because it didn't care about protecting amateurism—it cared about publishing video games—and in part because it knew that it had used players' images and likenesses without their permission. Back in 2012 EA sent us boxes of papers as part of a document request. In one of the boxes were email printouts. Among them were emails from EA Sports staff in which they talked about designing and coding the *March*

Madness 08 game to include players' names. But then, as those emails explained, EA pulled the names right before publication.

Why would EA do that?

Because the Collegiate Licensing Company—the exclusive trademark licensing agent for the NCAA—warned them to do so.

"This is exactly the type of thing that could submarine the game," CLC senior vice president Derek Eiler wrote in an email to EA, "if it got to the media."

Joel Linzer, an executive VP for EA, testified during our trial to provide additional details. He explained that EA had arrangements in place to easily negotiate with college athletes for a group license and that EA very much wanted those rights to make the games more realistic.

It was refreshing to hear Linzer's testimony. He made it clear that not only do college athletes' identity rights exist but they are undoubtedly valuable, too. That's true whether video game publishers, television networks, apparel companies, or a host of others in the college sports industry used those rights.

It's also worth noting that we never asked EA to stop making college sports games. Just the opposite, actually—we love EA Sports college games and wish EA still made them. All we asked for is that EA pursue what it really wanted to do: negotiate with us to use our identities.

So, no, my lawsuit hasn't stopped EA from publishing college sports video games. EA is simply afraid of the NCAA, which could decide not to allow the licensing of team and university intellectual property. If the NCAA told EA it could pay college athletes without retribution by the NCAA, we would see these college games. It's really that simple.

To be honest, the one disappointment I have from the lawsuit is that EA hasn't had the courage to say, "To hell with the NCAA!" EA has basically let the NCAA tell them what to do, and now consumers are being denied games that they clearly want. EA should reach out and negotiate a group license with players. We're more than willing, EA. It wouldn't cost you a lot, either—I can assure you. Most players would love to be in the video games. All they want is a small amount of money to show they count. It's really about respect.

Some would say EA figuring out how much money should go to each player would be complicated. Listen, we've flown to the moon. We've cured all sorts of diseases. I think figuring out a fair distribution of video game money is well within the abilities of mankind.

So, yes, EA should make a game with real college players, both current and past. If the NCAA won't license the schools, so be it. EA could use locations instead of those teams' names and other properties. College basketball video game players would probably be able to make an educated guess as to inspiration for that Washington, DC, college team with Patrick Ewing, Alonzo Mourning, Dikembe Mutombo, and Allen Iverson, all digitized and all real on the roster.

Look, the NCAA endorsed EA doing that kind of manipulation—and much more—to our identities as players, so I can't imagine the NCAA would object to it being done to them.

Yeah, right.

All I know is people would buy those video games. You don't need the NCAA for college sports and you don't need them for college sports video games, either.

As it's been said before, if you build it, they will come.

CHAPTER 12

THE WIN, THE APPEAL AND THE WAIT

It was Friday, August 8, 2014, around 2 p.m. when I found out. I was in a showroom, talking with customers, when my colleague, Cody Carter, walked up to me and said, "Ed, I've got to talk to you for a moment."

He took me aside and smiled. "Dude, you won!"

"Wait, what?"

"You beat the NCAA! It's all over the news, man!"

Cody is a bit of a jokester and I've fallen for a prank or two in my life—I mean, who hasn't? But he insisted that he wasn't messing with me.

"Man, check out the news—go to your computer. It's all over the internet, all over ESPN. Brother, I'm not lying. I swear."

At that point the emotions started to surface. This was real.

But I didn't know exactly how to feel.

I ran over to one of our showroom TVs and put on ESPN: BREAKING NEWS: COURT RULES FOR ED O'BANNON. NCAA LOSES. And the hosts were talking about the case.

Boom!

And how about that? We really had won!

Then I ran to my computer like I was sprinting for an alley-oop pass from Tyus Edney. I wanted to read everything possible about our win. I wanted to soak it in and breathe easy.

And I did, to an extent. The thing is, the law seems to go out of its way to be complex. As I learned, there's a lot to unwind in a legal decision.

In reading other people's reactions to Judge Wilken's order, I quickly realized that there was real confusion about what she had actually ruled.

Now, we clearly had won—we proved the NCAA was in violation of federal antitrust law in using the names, images, and likenesses of current and former Division I football and basketball players without negotiating with players for that use.

No court had ever made that proclamation until now. Someone was finally calling out the NCAA for breaking the law and for doing us wrong. And the voice ruling against the NCAA was that of a federal judge.

But some journalists and bloggers disagreed about Judge Wilken's remedy. They didn't understand the idea of a trust and a $5,000 per-year limit.

It's not an obvious remedy, and there was a complicated path taken to get to it.

Michael and Sathya had told me that proving that the NCAA had broken the law and forcing the NCAA to change its rules were related but nonetheless two very different things.

A lawsuit is not only about proving the illegality of the other side's actions, it's also about convincing the judge that a proposed fix to the situation is the way to go. A proposed solution should make the folks who are suing "whole again," at least to the extent that the law and money can actually do that.

So I knew that if Judge Wilken agreed with us about the NCAA behaving unlawfully—which she most definitely did—she would then have to decide what to do about it.

But there was another layer, Michael and Sathya warned. Judge Wilken didn't want to impose a remedy that the NCAA could easily appeal to the appellate court.

Like a coach designing a play that anticipates how the other side would react, Judge Wilken had to anticipate how the NCAA and appellate judges would respond to the remedy she ordered. She wanted a ruling that would be appeal-proof. Otherwise, the appellate court would reverse, which means our celebration would be short-lived.

With that in mind, Judge Wilken navigated a range of options for a remedy.

She could have ordered the NCAA to change its amateurism rules immediately to allow for compensation for college athletes and also allow those athletes to hire agents to do their bidding.

As part of that change, the NCAA, conferences, colleges, apparel companies, and anyone else in the business of profiting off the identities of football and men's basketball players would need to begin negotiations with current and former players for the current and future use of their names, images, and likenesses. And she could have required the NCAA to pay a lot of money in damages for the past use, too. This kind of remedy would have been the whole ball of wax—the knockout blow, if you will.

Michael and Sathya were skeptical that Judge Wilken would do anything like that. We hadn't explicitly asked for that kind of sweeping remedy. Plus, as they explained, the more extensive or disruptive the remedy, the more vulnerable it could be on appeal.

As a slightly different alternative, Judge Wilken could have imposed a similarly sweeping fix but provided the NCAA with a good amount of time—months or even years—to gradually get its act together.

That would have been more realistic than everything changing at once, but it was still unlikely. Judges, I hear, often don't like to be game changers; they prefer to fix a problem in the most confined way possible.

So we thought Judge Wilken would probably opt for a more narrowly defined and cautious remedy.

We obviously would have preferred a complete takedown of amateurism—we still do—but that's not what our case was ever about. We sued so that college athletes would get a fair say over the use of their names, images, and likenesses—and that's really it. Anything else would have been gravy.

This mission was always on our minds during the trial as my lawyers consistently suggested the idea of a "group-license model." This model is used in pro sports and it involves all of the athletes in a league collectively licensing their names, images, and likenesses for use in live game telecasts, video games, game rebroadcasts, advertisements, and archival footage. Although current and former college players could opt out of the group and hire an agent to do their negotiations, our thinking was (and is) that almost every player would remain in it.

Listen, college athletes are tremendously busy with sports and school. Probably almost every one of them would be okay with an association of college athletes doing all the negotiations. This kind of group-license approach would not be as disruptive to the culture and business of college sports as would the more extensive remedies mentioned above.

Now, we realized that college players couldn't unionize since the law does not (yet) recognize college players as employees. So, we weren't arguing specifically for that. That is a separate fight.

Instead, we envisioned a trade association—which is similar

to a union but its members don't have to be employees—negotiating a group license on college players' behalf. The trade association would deal with the NCAA, colleges, conferences, media companies, and others that want to use players' names, images, and likenesses.

There was still a chance, though, that Judge Wilken might find a group-license approach too impactful on college sports and, by extension, too disruptive of college life in general. We didn't see it as such, but reasonable minds can disagree here.

We wanted to provide Judge Wilken with an alternative. And it would be one that signaled that we were comfortable with players receiving fair compensation for the use of their names, images, and likenesses *after* their time in college ends—so long as their benefits accrued *during* college. Under this proposal, schools would hold payments in a trust and the money would be distributed to players after college. Payments would be equal among each player on a team.

The idea of a trust seemed to have traction during the trial, in part because of comments made by the people who testified for the NCAA.

Neal Pilson, the former president of CBS Sports and a Yale Law School alumnus, was supposed to be the NCAA's star witness. At least, that is what we heard. The thought was that he'd convince Judge Wilken that TV companies don't need to negotiate with players for their names, images, and likenesses because students don't control media access to the arenas and stadia where games are played. In other words, in Pilson's view, college athletes have no protected interest in their image being broadcast because they have no say over whether they are broadcast and that's because only their schools decide whether the broadcast will happen.

Got it? It was some all-star-level circular reasoning! Basically, college athletes get no pay because they have no say.

Well he wasn't convincing—either to Judge Wilken or to us.

During cross-examination, Pilson admitted to Bill Isaacson that his analysis falls apart in certain situations. Pilson acknowledged that TV networks needed to negotiate with visiting teams even though those teams have no control over access to arenas and stadia.

Plus, Pilson admitted that network contracts carry extensive language about identity rights—including name, image, and likeness—and yet the "persons" mentioned in those contracts weren't able to negotiate. To that end, Pilson was asked to explain why the Big 12 and Fox had signed a contract in 2011 that contained this "grants of rights" clause:

> The Conference shall be solely responsible for securing all clearances with respect to all officials and other persons participating in or otherwise connected with each Event, and such clearances shall include FOX having all rights or consents necessary or contemplated for the exercise of their rights under this Agreement, including, without limitation, all name and likeness rights of all participants, officials, competing teams and any other persons connected with the Events that are reasonable or necessary for the Telecast of the Events and the promotion and advertising thereof.

Now, I'm no lawyer, but I see the words *name* and *likeness* and *rights* in that clause. And so did Judge Wilken! And we'll be damned if "persons participating in or otherwise connected with each Event" doesn't include the players.

Look, even fans attending games see their identity rights recognized as part of the production. Game tickets—which are contracts—normally contain language about the use of spectators' voices, images, and likenesses in the broadcast. It is only players whose identity rights are taken as automatically owned by the school.

Pilson also made a remark that unintentionally paved the way for our victory. Toward the end of Pilson's testimony, Isaacson picked apart Pilson's claim that college fans would lose their interest in college sports if the players were paid. Pilson even threw out the hypothetical that if each Boston College basketball player were paid $200,000 for the use of his name, image, and likeness on TV broadcasts it would turn off Boston College Eagles fans.

First off, I don't agree with Pilson on that point and there's no independent data that supports it. Would Eagles supporters be so upset that the players are getting their fair share—or really any share—of the value being made off their names, images, and likenesses that they would no longer be fans?

Even if we lived in an illogical world and Pilson was correct, he set himself up to fail by throwing out a number—$200,000—because it implies that the reaction of fans would be different if the dollar figure were lower.

Bill Isaacson pounded on the opportunity like Michael Jordan seeing open air to fly. He demanded that Pilson apply his so-called logic to a different hypothetical: one in which players would receive a lower dollar amount. It appeared that Pilson was caught off guard. He looked almost annoyed. I thought to myself, *Man, I bet he wishes he never offered the BC basketball hypothetical.*

Pilson first said that he couldn't offer a figure because "it would depend on which team and how much money is being allocated." Then he uttered sixteen words that I felt bolstered our case: "I'd tell you $1 million would trouble me and $5,000 wouldn't. That's a pretty good range." So, in other words, the NCAA's own witness opined that players being paid $5,000 a year in a trust would be fine.

Wait a second. I thought amateurism only works if there is *no* pay? Now we find out that amateurism works so long as the pay is $5,000.

This wasn't amateurism. This was amateur hour.

While Pilson's remarks stood out, he wasn't the only NCAA witness to say or imply that players being paid would be compatible with amateurism. Bernard Muir, the Stanford athletic director whom I discussed earlier, testified that players being paid "six figures, seven figures" would "concern" him. Why wouldn't *any* figure be concerning if amateurism is so essential to college sports?

Likewise, Dr. John Dennis, the NCAA's survey expert, had testified that while some fans would be turned off by players being paid, it would depend on how much money they are being paid.

Again, the NCAA's own witnesses talked openly about a correlation between how much money players are paid and consumer interest in the NCAA. In doing so, they signaled that not all amounts of money are worrisome to the NCAA's popularity. This meant there was really no justification for players to receive zero dollars for colleges' use of their names, images, and likenesses. Obviously, some amount of money was okay to the NCAA.

Judge Wilken seized on this point in her opinion. She reasoned that schools and conferences should be able to "make limited payments to student-athletes above the cost of attendance," for doing so would—in the NCAA's own admission—cause the NCAA no legal harm.

She picked Pilson's $5,000 amount as the limit of those payments for every year that the student-athlete remains academically eligible to compete and stressed that the payments could only occur after players had finished playing college sports. As a result, the NCAA was ordered to change its amateurism rules to allow for such payments. The ruling, though, was not set to go into effect for another year and after the appeals.

Was $5,000 the right number? I'm not sure. It seemed to be based on Pilson's off-the-cuff remark. But I was still thrilled to see it. Players would get something. And something is a lot closer to fairness than nothing.

I called Michael and Sathya to get their thoughts, but neither was available. I talked to one of their secretaries, however, and she said, "We're trying to get ahold of Michael but he is at a play in New York City."

I also called Rosa as she was picking up Edward from school. She was ecstatic. So was my boss, Rich Abajian. By the time I saw him, I was bouncing off the walls. He told me congratulations, and then said, "Ed, you should go home. Go celebrate. Get out of here and enjoy this moment. You earned it."

At about that time, Michael's assistant got in touch with him, and he called me. We talked about how we won, but Michael stressed that there was an appeal ahead. "We got off on the right foot," Michael said calmly—the man is always calm. "But soon comes the appeal, Ed. You might just say we're going into overtime." I loved that Michael, who doesn't know much about sports, threw in the "overtime" reference. He made such an effort to learn about college sports culture—which was foreign to him prior to the trial. Those efforts paid off.

Mr. and Mrs. Vaccaro then called me. They started reading portions of the decision. It was sweet justice, sweet justice. They loved that Judge Wilken agreed with us that the NCAA had illegally prevented players and former players from compensation for the use of their names, images, and likenesses. As Mr. Vaccaro kept repeating, Judge Wilken didn't buy the NCAA's theories that noncompensation for those rights was necessary for amateurism. It felt so good to hear Judge Wilken's words spoken through Mr. Vaccaro. It was as if those words were meant to be told in his narration.

My phone kept getting calls and texts. It was a day to remember, that's for sure.

When I got home, Rosa and Edward had popped open a bottle of champagne. We celebrated the victory. But I was exhausted, too. I really didn't want to do any media interviews. I just wanted to enjoy the moment with my family. I was just like, this is done, let's celebrate together, and then let's move on. We got what we wanted. Savor it tonight and then get ready for the next game.

Mr. Vaccaro, however, called me and basically said, "Eddie, you have to do one radio interview with ESPN. You can't go silent. We won and you need to get out there." So I did one interview in between sipping drinks with Rosa. That was really it on the night we won.

But the interview requests wouldn't stop. I knew this was a big deal and I had to give the case its due. I agreed to take an hour out of work the next day to do a small press conference in a conference room at Findlay. ESPN was there, but it was more for the local news media. It was a chance to talk to everyone at the same time, which made my life easier.

Then Sunday came. The dealership was closed, and Rosa and I did like we usually do on Sundays: relax. We went to the movies. Then we had a family barbeque in the back yard. We chilled out. That's really what we do in the O'Bannon household on Sundays—even those Sundays right after we beat the NCAA.

Keeping my home and family life as separate from the case as I reasonably could was essential. During the entire lawsuit, we treated every day as a normal day. There was not one time when I brought the case home. We never talked about it at the dinner table. Not once. My kids may have seen the lawsuit cause me stress, but we largely kept it out of the house. And, look, my kids didn't ask for their dad to sue the NCAA and be on ESPN and all that. It was my deal and I kept it that way.

For that reason, we never allowed a media interview in our house. Trust me, there were many requests to do sit-downs with the family. No thanks. I respect their work, but no reporters are allowed in our home. It's our world and it's staying that way.

That was the attitude I held as the weeks and months passed

before the next stage of the legal process. As expected, the NCAA quickly appealed Judge Wilken's ruling to the US Court of Appeals for the Ninth Circuit. A hearing date was set for March 17, 2015, and it would take place in the James R. Browning US Courthouse in San Francisco.

I knew the appeal hearing would be a completely different ballgame from the trial. One major difference was that I would not be testifying again. In fact, I'd play no role whatsoever. As my lawyers explained to me, appeals are only about questions of law. The Ninth Circuit Court wouldn't be revisiting the facts or anything like that. They would take the record of facts as determined by Judge Wilken and defer to it.

This was a positive factor for us. Judge Wilken's findings showed that the NCAA clearly profited off our names, images, and likenesses and that we didn't receive a dime. There would be no witness testimony that might cloud the truth. The same would be true of any attempts by the NCAA to introduce new "evidence" that distracts from reality. None of that could, or would, happen.

Victory wasn't assured, however. A three-judge panel on the Ninth Circuit would review how Judge Wilken understood the law and how she applied it to her factual findings. It was conceivable that we could have proven that the NCAA had ripped off current and former college athletes but not have proven, in the eyes of the Ninth Circuit, that the NCAA had violated the law. This was worrisome.

So was the fact that the NCAA brought in the big guns for the appeal. They hired the former US Solicitor General, Seth Waxman, to deliver their arguments before the three-judge Ninth Circuit panel. I guess the NCAA figured their system of amateurism was on the line, so they'd better go all out and bring in a ringer.

And it would all be decided after just one hearing in court.

This was another major difference between a trial and an appeal. A trial is kind of like a seven-game NBA playoff series. Each day is a new matchup and the winner of game one might not win game two. Rarely is the outcome a sweep. An appeal, in contrast, is much more like the NCAA championship game. Everything gets decided in one matchup. An attorney for one side gets about a half hour to present and answer some pretty aggressive questions by the three judges. And then the other attorney goes.

And then everyone goes home and waits for a decision by the judges.

Needless to say, both sides in an appellate oral argument leave nothing on—or maybe I should say "in"—the court. If it's not your day, you make it your day. You have to, or you lose.

Michael and the other lawyers told me I didn't need to attend the oral argument, but man, I knew I had to be there. Look, my name is on this. I have to be there. I want to be there. In some small way, too, I felt like my being there set the right tone for our side. I mean, how do I not go? After all these years in court, what in my life is going to keep me away? I didn't want people asking questions as to why I wasn't there. That would do us no good.

I think they noticed me sitting there in the second row—each of the judges made eye contact with me at several points during the hearing. Their clerks did, too. Now, sure, I stand out. There weren't any other six-foot-eight black guys in the courtroom that day. But I could tell they knew who I was. They looked at me more than anyone else sitting around me.

It's like playing in a game and certain people sitting in the audience stand out. Your eyes roll across the sea of fans, and suddenly someone familiar captures your attention. Sometimes it's a family member or a friend. Sometimes it's just someone famous. At Lakers games, you can bet that Magic, Kobe, and Shaq all noticed Jack Nicholson sitting in his courtside seat. They may not admit it, but they saw him. They took stock of him wearing his sunglasses and flashing his distinctive smile. These days, Lonzo Ball is doing the exact same thing. He may not be old enough to know Nicholson's films, but you can bet Lonzo notices Nicholson.

Some people in the audience just stand out.

I remember when we played the University of Kentucky in the John Wooden Classic back in December of 1994. It was a marquee game—Kentucky was ranked number three at the time and we were number five—and it would be televised nationally. The game was also played at the Honda Center in Anaheim. That arena seated nearly nineteen thousand people. This was a big-time college basketball matchup. In one of the courtside seats right next to the scorer's table sat Arsenio Hall. Now, he wasn't pumping his fists yelling, "Roo, Roo, Roo!" like on his TV show. But he was there. And we all kept looking over to him.

I think we tend to notice the faces that we should notice. It's something about the way our minds work. It's like we gravitate toward certain people in the crowd.

I felt like my face should have been noticed in Courtroom 1 of the James R. Browning US Courthouse. This lawsuit had my name on it. I may not have had a role in the hearing, but I would be doing my side a disservice if I weren't there.

The hearing began by Waxman delivering what seemed like a speech written by Mark Emmert. The three judges, Chief Judge Sidney Thomas, Judge Jay Bybee, and Judge Gordon Quist, all listened attentively.

It was a different dynamic from the trial in Judge Wilken's courtroom. For one, the courtroom in San Francisco was much larger and way more decorative, with marble columns, stone pillars, and a vaulted ceiling. There were inscribed seals throughout the room. It felt like it was a courtroom for the elite, to be honest. Also, the three decision makers were from a different walk of life than Judge Wilken. All three of them were older white guys and, for whatever it's worth, two of them—Judges Bybee and Quist—had been appointed by Republican presidents. There was more formality in how they talked, too. They seemed to be more about custom than Judge Wilken was. This dynamic was a little bit concerning for me. My case is fundamentally about change and disruption whereas these judges seemed more about maintaining order.

For his part, Waxman began by asserting a point I disagree with. "Amateur athletics," Waxman claimed, "long predated the NCAA's founding in 1905 for the purpose of extending to intercollegiate sports its defining principle: that athletes must not be paid."

That's not my understanding of why the NCAA was founded. The NCAA was created out of necessity. Back then, President Theodore Roosevelt had expressed concerns about college athletes dying. He threatened to federally regulate college sports unless colleges got their act together. Fearful of regulation, college presidents formed the NCAA and passed safety rules, promising to make college sports safe.

The NCAA wasn't about amateurism when it was founded and didn't care about it until schools realized how much money they could earn from college athletes. In fact, the phrase *student-athlete* didn't even come into existence until after World War II. And it was used by NCAA lawyers when they argued before judges and state industrial commissions that colleges shouldn't have to pay workers' compensation to seriously injured football players—you know, the very players the NCAA was created to protect fifty years earlier!

I get that Waxman was a paid advocate for the NCAA. His job was to convince the three judges that Judge Wilken was wrong. But to listen to one position after another that I disagreed with and not be able to stand up in court and say, "Yo, I disagree!" was hard.

Waxman went on, saying that college athletes can't be paid any portion of a "specific commercial revenue stream" or they wouldn't be amateurs. Talk about convenient logic. The NCAA comes up with a definition of amateurism so that it can keep all of the money.

Judge Thomas was clearly skeptical of Waxman, especially when Waxman claimed that "there is an NCAA rule dealing with NIL rights." Thomas responded that no, name-image-likeness rights *are* referenced in TV and other contracts. Remember the trial?

Michael Hausfeld was then up. He stressed that despite what the NCAA claims, the NCAA is actually subject to antitrust laws and must be competitive in how it imposes rules on college athletes. It was a basic, logical point, yet one that the NCAA can't seem to grasp.

But Michael took fire from the judges too. Judge Thomas, who earlier seemed to doubt Waxman, was just as disbelieving of Michael. And Judge Quist chimed in with some skeptical questions as well. I was struck by how frequently the judges interrupted both lawyers. I later learned that it's relatively common in an appellate hearing, but it's still jarring to see for the first time.

On balance, Michael seemed to be more of a target of the judges' skepticism than Waxman seemed to be in the courtroom this day. Judge Thomas, for instance, kept asking Michael about whether the fact that EA had stopped making college video games rendered the lawsuit moot.

Michael powerfully responded that the absence of the video games missed the point. The point was that the NCAA's rules made it impossible for colleges and conferences to compensate college athletes for their names, images, and likenesses. Those rules also made it impossible for those colleges and conferences to compete with each other in negotiating video game deals and in negotiating to pay college athletes for use of their names, images, and likenesses.

By the time the hearing ended, about an hour and a half had passed. I felt very different from how I felt after we left Judge Wilken's courtroom for the final time. I don't know if I had a certain look on my face, but I had an altogether different feeling in my gut. Although the judges showed hostility to both sides, it seemed like they saved their greatest aggression for Michael. It was like they didn't understand what he was saying or simply disagreed with him.

As we walked out, I could tell we didn't have that fire in our eyes. I sensed things were starting to change for us and not in a good way.

We found a private corner in the hallway where we were huddled together, and I decided to speak up. Rosa says I tend to wear my emotions on my sleeve. I certainly did at that moment. Then I asked, to no one in particular but within earshot of Michael, Sathya, and the Vaccaros, "What the hell just happened in there?" They were like, "Don't worry about it, Ed—it's just part of the process." I wasn't convinced. "Are you serious?" I snapped back. "Really, what just happened in there? Are they going to overturn this? Did everything we worked so hard to accomplish over the years just get thrown into the trash?"

They continued to assure me not to worry, but I could read it in their body language. I could see it in their eyes. I could hear it in the tone of their voices. The hearing hadn't gone the way they wanted.

Even if they wouldn't say it, they feared we were going to lose the appeal. And waiting for the appellate court decision weighed on me more than I anticipated. I didn't think it would take so long for them to decide.

That feeling of monotony and repetition brought me back to my days in the NBA.

• • •

We're twelve chapters into the book and I haven't yet talked about my NBA career. That's somewhat by design, as it does reflect the fact that my time in the NBA was a less than wonderful chapter in my life.

My game, which thrived in college, didn't translate as well as I had hoped in the NBA. Persistent knee problems didn't help either.

But there's much more to tell.

You see, I got off to a bad start with the Nets' head coach, Butch Beard, when the Nets training camp opened in September 1995. Butch was well known as a "veterans' coach" in that he preferred to play experienced players even if that meant slowing the development of younger players. He certainly lived up to that reputation. Butch had been a longtime assistant NBA coach who, after running the show at Howard University in the early '90s, finally got a break to become an NBA coach in 1994. He knew that if this opportunity didn't turn out well, it might very well be his last.

By the time I arrived, Butch was on a short leash with Nets management, too. A year earlier, he had coached the Nets to a 30–52 record. It was the franchise's worst record in years, and the team finished in second-to-last place in the Atlantic Division. He had to win in 1995 or he would be shown the door.

Butch knew that the way to win in the NBA is with veterans, not rookies. At the same time, I was a lottery pick, and our general manager, Willis Reed, had a vested stake in seeing me succeed—Reed needed to prove that he had made the right choice in selecting me instead of other players like Gary Trent and Corliss Williamson. So, Butch couldn't ignore me. Even if he didn't want to play me, he knew his boss thought otherwise.

The result was a coach who was constantly frustrated by his rookie lottery pick, someone he didn't want to play but felt compelled to. Butch just didn't have a whole lot of patience for me in particular and for rookie mistakes in general.

Now, I was aware of this dynamic before the season started. And I hoped to overcome it by trying to hit the ground running. And initially, I thought I accomplished that. I played well at the very start of training camp and seemed to fit the offense.

But then my knee swelled up and I missed about half of training camp. I basically lived in the training room.

So right off the bat I'm sure Butch was thinking, *We drafted a guy who can't get out of the training room.* Even though I recovered from the knee swelling by early in the season, from that point on it was an uphill climb for me with Butch.

Worse yet, I wasn't meeting the heavy expectations placed on me by the franchise and its fans. The Nets had marketed me as a guy who would contribute from day one and the media bought into that narrative.

From the New Jersey Nets program.
(Courtesy of Brooklyn Sports & Entertainment)

It wasn't a crazy idea, either. Unlike players who had jumped to the NBA straight out of high school or after one year of college, I had played four full seasons of NCAA ball. Relative to other rookies, I had a ton of experience under my belt. And at twenty-three years old, I was kind of an "old" rookie.

I remember someone handed me a copy of a *New York Times* article about me. It read, "The Nets believe the 6-foot-8 forward will make sweet music in the open floor with Kenny Anderson and Derrick Coleman." It also described how I would help to "turn around the franchise."

It just didn't work out that way. After being an elite shooter in college, I struggled to make my shots in the NBA, where the players are so much more skilled on the defensive end. And unlike in college, when Coach Harrick would keep me in a game until I got my groove, Coach Beard wouldn't hesitate to yank me and sit me on the bench.

I also couldn't find a rhythm when my playing time was so erratic. One night I would play fifteen minutes. The next night I would get thirty-two minutes. Then in the following game I'm down to five minutes again. I wasn't the only player on the team whose playing time fluctuated in ways that didn't seem to have any rhyme or reason. But as a rookie, you have no prior NBA experiences to draw from, so it's easy to feel discouraged.

And as a team, we struggled mightily. We started out 4–8 in our first 12 games and never rebounded. We ended up finishing in last place in the Atlantic Division. My play didn't help matters. I went from a guy who shot 53 percent in college to one who couldn't crack 40 percent. The only person who I could blame for missing shots was myself. I took them and I missed them. We also had our fair share of acrimony in the locker room. An NBA season lasts a long time, especially when you lose more than you win. It's natural that players will eventually start pointing fingers over why everything is turning out wrong. The whole experience was terribly frustrating. I had never gone through anything like it. I had always played on winning or at least competitive teams.

It wasn't entirely bad, though. I had a great mentor in my teammate Rick Mahorn. He was thirty-seven years old and had played in the league for sixteen seasons. If he saw that I was down, he'd put his arms around me. He would call me in the middle of the night to make sure I was good. A few times he went out of his way to comfort me and give me advice. Rick Mahorn was my man.

Another highlight took place when I played against Michael Jordan for the first time. In November of 1995, we traveled to play the Bulls in Chicago. This was the Bulls team that would go on to win seventy-two games, the most regular-season wins of any NBA team until the Warriors won seventy-three in 2016. Man, it was like playing against celebrities! Jordan and Pippen were unreal. They had such incredible chemistry on the court and they were mighty tough to defend as well. I thought I had Jordan contained on one play but then he pivoted quickly and blew by me. Those guys are obviously legends now, but they were legends then too.

Still, playing with Rick Mahorn and playing against Jordan were rare highlights in an otherwise dismal rookie season. The season also ended with an embarrassing loss in Atlanta. The Hawks beat us by twenty-two points. Might as well have been fifty-two points. I sat on the bench and watched with torn ligaments in my shooting hand. I couldn't wait to get out of there. I couldn't wait to get home, to be honest.

A few days after the Hawks loss, Willis Reed fired Butch Beard. That was it for Butch. He would never again be an NBA head coach. In the offseason, the Nets hired John Calipari, who'd had a phenomenal coaching career at UMass. The hiring brought new hope for the franchise but also uncertainty for the players, including me. We knew Coach Cal would want to bring in his own guys, if not at the start then as time went on.

Coach Cal did reach out to me when he got into town in June. We went out to lunch. I enjoyed our conversation. He is a fun and very charismatic guy. He was also candid about how I needed to improve my game, especially in terms of taking better shots and, of course, making those shots. He made clear that he expected I would be a key contributor.

Coach Cal also left me with the impression that I was going to play more of my natural position, the "four," or power forward, which is what I played in college. During my rookie year Coach Beard tended to play me at the "three" (small forward), thinking that my size was a better fit for that position.

But the problem with the small forward position in the NBA is that the defenders at that position tend to be super quick and it's very hard to generate your own shot against them. Power forwards, in contrast, tend to be bigger but also slower than small forwards. With a return to my natural position, I felt optimistic for the first time in my Nets career.

From June to October I tried to bulk up as much as possible in anticipation of playing power forward in the following season. I thought I would play down low more and get closer to the basket and grab more rebounds. I went to training camp a lot heavier, but the added weight was muscle.

Then the 1996–97 season started, and I really didn't have a defined position. Coach Cal didn't seem to have a lot of confidence in me either. I wasn't sure what had changed from when I had met him for lunch a few months earlier. It may have been that management had added several veteran forwards—Xavier McDaniel and Tony Massenburg—to the mix and I simply fell down the depth chart as a result. Or maybe Calipari was blowing smoke in my ear and he never intended to play me. I really don't know.

Either way, I didn't help matters on my end. I continued to shoot the ball poorly. I couldn't figure out why—I was missing the kind of open shots that I had consistently made in college. And once I started to miss shots, I started to think about missing shots and it impacted my timing. So I started to miss more shots. It became a vicious cycle and I wound up on the bench again.

With that in mind, it shouldn't have surprised me when the trade happened, but it nonetheless shocked me.

I was in my condo on February 17, 1997. I lived by myself, as Rosa had stayed in California with her business. Both Rosa and my mom had visited and made it feel like home, but I never felt like it was my home, even though I lived there for a couple of years.

Anyway, it was the day of the NBA's trading deadline, the last day teams could make trades until the offseason.

My phone rang and Coach Cal was on the other line. He told me, "Hey, Ed, I have some news for you."

"Sure thing, Coach, what's happening?"

"Well, you've been traded to the Dallas Mavericks, Ed. I want you to know that it was a lot of fun to coach you. I wish you good luck. I think this will be a great opportunity for you. And I have no doubt I will see you again down the line."

Not much was said in the conversation. Then again, not a whole lot needed to be said.

The idea of a trade wasn't necessarily a bad thing for me, either. A change of scenery might have been just what the doctor ordered. It couldn't really get worse than my situation with the Nets.

Or could it?

The Nets had traded me to the Dallas Mavericks, whose top assistant coach was…you guessed it, Butch Beard. Of all coaches, it had to be him, didn't it? We didn't mesh at all in New Jersey and I knew we wouldn't in Dallas either.

So it wasn't surprising that I was immediately relegated to the bench in Dallas. I only played in nineteen games. And when I played, it was usually for only a handful of minutes and in garbage time.

The Mavericks didn't seem very invested in my future, either. This was sort of expected, and it didn't bother me all that much. The Nets had used a lottery pick to draft me and thus had a clear stake in my development. It was a completely different story with the Mavericks. I was more of a trade "throw-in" to them. The Mavericks acquired me from the Nets in a trade in which the centerpiece acquisition was seven-foot-six center Shawn Bradley, who was a heck of a player and a great person, too.

I was really no longer lottery pick Ed O'Bannon. With the Mavericks, I had become random guy #31 O'Bannon at the end of the bench. A guy you trust to play during blowouts but that's about it.

I almost felt like I had regressed to when I was a freshman backup on the Verbum Dei High School varsity team. I was on the roster but playing time was scarce.

Seven months later the Mavericks traded me to the Orlando Magic. I was a throw-in to a deal involving Derrick Harper, Dennis Scott, and $500,000 in cash. I basically helped to make the financial numbers work under the NBA salary-cap system, which limits how much each team can spend on player salaries. In other words, my contract was really being traded, not me.

The Magic would waive me a month after that. I ended up playing 128 games in the NBA. I wish it had lasted longer.

My whole time in the NBA was really a blur. I never got comfortable. My timing, my thought process, everything was just off. My whole life I had been a star but then I became a disappointment. A bust. A failure. I didn't know how to handle it. And, maybe worse, I didn't know how to fix it. No one else around me did either. I always felt like I had one foot out the door of the league, with the other foot ready to follow.

And let me be clear: I don't blame anyone but myself. Like I said earlier, I took those shots and I missed them.

But I'd be lying if I said I never think about how my NBA career could have turned out differently if a different NBA team had drafted me.

Sometimes I think about those cheers we heard from the Toronto fans in the SkyDome on draft night. "WE WANT ED! WE WANT ED! WE WANT ED!"

Other times I imagine if the Portland Trailblazers had taken me with the number-eight pick. I wouldn't have been far from my family. The transition to life as a Trailblazer would have been so much easier. And the Trailblazers' coach, P.J. Carlesimo, had been a longtime college coach who I know admired my game.

But that's not how life worked out. The NBA draft doesn't send you where you want to go. It sends you where you *will* go, and it's up to you to make the best of it.

And as I waited for the Ninth Circuit to make a decision, I thought back to that. Sometimes you've got to go with the flow.

CHAPTER 13

VICTORY AT LAST

THE BIG WAIT WOULD COME TO AN END—SORT OF—ON Wednesday, September 30, 2015. I had just shown a customer a Toyota Avalon and felt optimistic that I would secure a sale. It was at that moment when word began to trickle in: the Ninth Circuit had issued the ruling, and I had won—again—but the $5,000 figure that Judge Wilken had imposed was removed.

I headed over to my computer to learn more. There was a lot to unpack.

I was very happy, and frankly relieved, to see that the Ninth Circuit had upheld Judge Wilken's ruling. The Ninth Circuit agreed that the NCAA violated antitrust law by conspiring to prevent current and former players from negotiating for the use of their names, images, and likenesses. The central argument in our case had withstood appellate scrutiny. Our fight had prevailed, which was no sure thing after that uncomfortable hearing in March.

The bottom line, then, was a good one: we had proved that the NCAA violated the law. And, man, did that feel sweet.

But the NCAA tried to frame the win as a hollow one, and it courted friendly media to advance that narrative.

In ruling for us, the Ninth Circuit concluded that the appropriate remedy was for the NCAA to allow schools to offer college athletes up to the "full cost of attendance" for the right to use their names, images, and likenesses. This is a dollar figure set by the federal government and is normally in the $2,500-to-$5,000 range. Full cost of attendance varies by school and reflects different costs and prices depending on where a student attends college. The amount is paid while the athlete is enrolled in college, meaning it is not part of a trust for deferred payment.

The NCAA got word out that it was only being ordered to do what it had already decided to do. A year earlier, the NCAA had adopted a rule that permitted schools to offer the full cost of attendance. So the NCAA framed the Ninth Circuit's ruling as inconsequential.

No, my friends, we *had* won and it *would* matter.

First off, let's remember the past correctly. The NCAA didn't approve the full cost of attendance in 2015 in a vacuum. It did so in response to our lawsuit, which, it's worth recalling, we had filed in 2009. Without our lawsuit—or without someone else bringing a similar case—there's no question that the NCAA wouldn't have agreed to this reform. It's no state secret that the NCAA *never* reforms unless it is forced to. We put their backs against the wall and led them to change.

Second, our lawsuit led to a settlement with EA that led to real dollars being paid to college athletes. About twenty-five thousand current and former college athletes have received checks averaging around $1,600. Sure, that kind of money won't make them rich, but it does make them feel that justice has taken place—and justice is truly priceless. The EA settlement wouldn't have happened without our case.

Third, and maybe most important of all, we won what I had originally sued for. I won for former players, who can now rely on my victory as precedent and bring their own cases against the NCAA, conferences, and schools and their various business partners. By doing so, former players will be able to collect money for the unauthorized use of their names, images, and likenesses.

One former player, ex–Ohio State linebacker Chris Spielman, has already brought such a case. In July 2017, Spielman filed a lawsuit in an Ohio federal court arguing that Ohio State and IMG College—the marketing company that negotiates on behalf of NCAA members—have unlawfully profited off his name and likeness, as well as those of other former Buckeye stars. They've done so by licensing those former players' identity rights to Honda in the carmaker's sponsored banners that are displayed throughout Ohio Stadium.

This is exactly the kind of practice I sued over: schools and businesses making money off former players without their consent or compensation.

Now, I've never met Chris Spielman or talked with him. I don't know the man at all. But I read his complaint and was excited to see it cited my victory: "Despite the holdings in the *O'Bannon v. NCAA* [case]," Spielman's complaint states, "OSU has entered into various licensing partnerships that unlawfully utilize the images of Plaintiff and Class Members."

Right on, Chris, right on!

Our victory has also strengthened ongoing cases against the NCAA. We've seen this a couple of times.

Take what happened in February 2017. It didn't get a lot of fanfare or publicity, but the NCAA agreed to pay $209 million to about forty thousand people who played or have played Division I football, men's basketball, and women's basketball since March 2010. The payment was part of a settlement to resolve a class action lawsuit led by former West Virginia University running back Shawne Alston. Shortly before our trial, Alston sued under the same antitrust laws we used to demand back payments from the NCAA because the NCAA had prevented schools from offering the full cost of attendance. Judge Wilken presided over the case. In rulings, she signaled that given our victory, Alston would probably win too. So the NCAA decided not to rack up another loss and instead cut a deal.

The same might happen in an ongoing case also presided over by Judge Wilken. A few years ago, former Clemson football player Martin Jenkins and other players sued the NCAA and five major conferences using similar antitrust arguments that would later work for us. Jenkins—who has since been joined in the lawsuit by former Wisconsin basketball star Nigel Hayes—argues that the NCAA's capping athletic scholarships to tuition, room, board, books, and fees violates the law.

Their argument makes sense.

The reason why athletic scholarships are capped is that the NCAA and its many members—all of whom represent themselves as competitors—have joined hands to limit those scholarships. That's the reason, and don't let anyone tell you otherwise.

Now, we know those schools will say they're broke and that they couldn't afford to pay more in athletic scholarships.

Right.

It's funny how colleges are so destitute and yet they find ways to pay coaches millions of dollars a year. They also somehow, some way, manage to finance the construction of stadia, arenas, and training facilities that can cost hundreds of millions of dollars.

I guess it's good to be broke!

Colleges have agreed to spend their money on everyone except the actual players. Instead of competing for athletes through scholarships that reflect competition, they take that surplus and compete by offering the highest-paid coach or most expensive stadium or the swankiest uniforms.

Money in. Money out.

It's an economy that has made a lot of people rich off the backs of young men and young women.

Well, Jenkins and Hayes are now able to rely on our victory as precedent in their case. This is an especially powerful point since the presiding judge is Judge Wilken and any appeals would go before the Ninth Circuit.

I wouldn't be surprised to see the NCAA try to cut a deal with Jenkins and Hayes. If the NCAA loses here, we could see the end of athletic scholarships having any cap. Schools would then be able to offer star high school recruits six- or even seven-figure athletic scholarships. Basically, the free market would dictate what happens.

This highlights a key difference between the Jenkins/Hayes case and my case: while their victory would most benefit star athletes that "should" command a lot more money in athletic scholarships, my case was about getting something for everyone—star, starter, benchwarmer, you name it.

I could see the NCAA not wanting to lose again. They could propose to Jenkins/Hayes settlement terms that would let schools offer athletes more value in athletic scholarships. It might not be a free market, but it would be an arrangement more along the lines of what competition and fairness ought to produce.

I mean, colleges are competitors, right?

In the NCAA's universe, competition and collusion often seem one and the same.

No matter what happens in ongoing litigation, I expect other players to follow the likes of Spielman, Alston, Jenkins, and Hayes. Former players know that when they appear on stadium banners, trading cards, vintage jerseys, and the many other products that use former players' identities for profit the law now says, *Hold on a second.*

And to be honest, it wouldn't surprise me if we see prospective college players take on the system too. They may not be in video games, but they appear in all sorts of commercialized materials. They are also subjected to NCAA-imposed restrictions on how they're recruited by so-called competing schools. Antitrust law worked in our case. It can work in other ones, especially given the precedent we established.

It's almost surreal to think of all these issues and what might eventually become of them. The thing is, twenty-two years ago I didn't know how to attack anticompetitive and unfair ideas. They were just part of a system that chugged along without anyone challenging it. Now I am in that position. The fact that my family and I stood up for something bigger than us—I love it. We started the snowball. That, to me, is the best part of this whole thing.

And in case you're wondering, I don't give a damn about who gets credit. I care about promoting justice, fairness, and positive change. There will be other lawsuits that take the arguments we brought and apply them in different circumstances. I don't need to be remembered as "the guy who beat the NCAA" and forced it to change its rules. I just want to see those rules changed so that justice and fairness prevail. That's what will matter in the long run: not the *who* but the *what.*

So we won and others have and will follow. But our win wasn't final until the highest court in the land had its say. In the world of March Madness, there was still one more round to go after the Ninth Circuit.

The NCAA appealed to the United States Supreme Court, and we filed a brief as well.

I knew the odds of the Supreme Court taking the case were really slim. As I understand it, the Supreme Court only agrees to hear about 1 percent of cases, and usually when there is a split among the federal courts of appeals about an important legal issue. No such split existed in our case: we had won the first case of its kind and no other case had been brought.

A part of me wanted to fly to Washington, DC, and take a taxi right over to the Supreme Court. "Mr. O'Bannon goes to Washington," if you will. I wanted to walk up the steps of the Supreme Court Building. I wanted to sit in the courtroom. I wanted to hear the justices debate what had begun a decade earlier with me watching a video game.

I also felt like the Supreme Court should have the final say and resolve these issues once and for all. It was a historic case. And that wasn't because of me. It's because it impacted thousands of college students and former college students across the country. In fact, my lawyers had told me that if the Supreme Court didn't take it, we might see cases similar to mine brought to court in other parts of the country.

So despite the long odds, I thought the momentum of history would play a role. And if this had been a movie, you know what would have happened.

But it wasn't a movie. And there was no actual momentum.

In October 2016 the Supreme Court declined to review the case. And that was it.

My feeling at the time was truly ambivalence. On one hand, I was disappointed not to have the opportunity to take our case to the Supreme Court. I'd be lying if I said I didn't want to snag a "national" and "permanent" win for our movement. The only way to get there is through the Supreme Court.

On the other hand, I felt pretty relieved. I had emotionally moved on from the case by the fall of 2016. Rosa definitely felt the same way. We had advanced in our careers and taken on more responsibility at work. Plus, our children were older and in different phases of adulthood. We wanted to be there for them and for each other. Look, we gave a decade of our lives to the case and I'm thrilled we won it. But we didn't need another two years of litigation just to get the Supreme Court to agree with us. Closure is a good thing. It was time to take stock of what had happened and make plans for what lay ahead.

Besides, there are other fighters who will come along and grab the baton. Chris Spielman is one. Nigel Hayes is another. There will be others.

Hey, you've got to keep punching the bully to let him know you're there and that you're not backing down. I did that for a decade, but others will enter the ring.

As I look back on the case now, I feel energized about what's to come. There will be other cases, other ideas, other changes—my story is really part of a larger narrative that has lasted for decades and still has a long arc ahead.

This feeling of turning the page reminds me of how I felt at the end of my NBA career. Closure came at me, but I didn't let it get me down. It marked the beginning of the next phase in my basketball career, and one that I enjoyed a great deal more.

One of the many great things about a pro basketball career is that even when the NBA dream dies, you can make a very good living playing basketball in other leagues. And when that happened to me in the late '90s, my family's international adventure began and my love for basketball returned.

Many NBA fans thought I had disappeared from the game when, after the Magic cut me, I couldn't find another NBA team. But from 1998 to 2004 I played for teams in places like Trieste, Italy; Valladolid, Spain; and Warsaw, Poland. These teams paid me six figures, allowing for my family to live well and experience different cultures.

• • •

Right after the Magic cut me, I was hesitant to relocate my family's life and my basketball career to Europe. I knew that once I took that step, getting back to the NBA would be very difficult, and maybe even impossible. Guys who play abroad usually don't return. If you cross over, you need to be prepared for not coming back.

Remember, this was an era before NBA scouts could watch online videos of players. Back then, if you played abroad, you'd only occasionally be seen live by scouts affiliated with NBA teams. Maybe your game would be shown on grainy videos, but there was no guarantee of even that. So there was something of an "out of sight, out of mind" effect—once you left the NBA, the NBA tended to forget about you.

With that in mind, I thought it would make sense to stay in the United States and play in a minor league. I had been told that NBA scouts would be much more likely to see me play if I stuck around. My agent started exploring different opportunities for me to play ball in the United States.

In February 1998 I signed a contract with the La Crosse, Wisconsin, Bobcats of the Continental Basketball Association.

The days of chartered flights, five-star hotels, and five-figure biweekly paychecks were about to end. In their place would be bus trips, cheap motels, and a salary of about $1,500 per week. No more arenas with 20,000 fans watching, either. I would soon be playing in "civic centers" where, on a good night, 2,500 people would be in attendance.

Despite these more modest surroundings, I was really excited to play again. No more being a benchwarmer.

And I would be joining a team that had other guys like me: former first-round NBA draft picks who hadn't panned out for one reason or another. Acie Earl, Rumeal Robinson, and Tony Dumas—these guys knew the situation I was in because they were in the same boat. And we had a coach, Don Zierden, who believed we would dominate the CBA and attract the attention of NBA scouts.

We had some fun, to be sure. And I loved the fact that I actually played! Instead of watching games from the end of the bench, I was back to starting and playing regular minutes. It took me a few games to regain my groove, but I was soon scoring twenty points and grabbing ten boards a game.

It just felt good to play well again. My confidence was gradually coming back and I felt way more at ease. I was no longer "thinking" while I was playing. The days of making a split-second look over at the coach to see his facial reaction if I screwed up were long gone. I just played. That mindset helped me regain the form I had at UCLA.

But it didn't lead to calls from NBA teams. Not even one.

Even though I was only twenty-five years old at the time, I started to realize that I might be facing a new reality. Maybe the NBA had moved on from me. Maybe my last NBA game would be when I had played less than one meaningless minute in an otherwise unremarkable loss against the Seattle Supersonics on April 10, 1997.

Maybe that was it.

Within a year or so, I would become okay with that whole notion. But in February and March of 1998 I wasn't quite ready to accept it. I believed I had time to get back to the NBA and that I would get an opportunity to do so.

Well, while waiting in Wisconsin for a call from an NBA team that never came, my agent told me that Alma Trieste, an Italian team, had a roster spot available and they were curious about my interest.

Not only had this roster spot become open but it was also available to an American player—not a common occurrence.

In Europe, leagues have limits on the number of foreign players who can play on any given team. We don't do that in the United States. We don't say, *the Boston Celtics must have at least four American players or four guys from New England* or something like that. But in Europe, leagues believe that national restrictions help to encourage local interest in the sport and get more young people interested, too.

I should mention that the pay in Europe was (and still is) much better than in the Continental Basketball Association or other American minor leagues. In fact, back then it was common for an American in Europe to earn in the ballpark of $300,000 to $400,000 over a seven-month season. Not too shabby.

Trieste was also a solid team, which made them appealing. They were in first place in their division. I also liked that the commitment to play in Italy wouldn't be for very long. If I signed with Trieste, I would only be bound to play in the remaining eight games of their regular season and the postseason. I was basically signing up for a two-month stay. Psychologically, this was important since I hadn't yet given up on my NBA dream. I viewed Trieste as an opportunity to keep playing but for more money. It was kind of like a paid working vacation. I had every intention of returning to the NBA at the start of the '98–99 season.

Trieste it was. I signed on and moved there for a couple of months. I loved my life in Italy. For one, I played really well, averaging sixteen points and over ten rebounds a game. But the food was great too. The people were friendly. The entire experience was positive.

I returned to the United States after the Italian season ended, and my agent secured a tryout for me with the Miami Heat. This was particularly exciting since Pat Riley was their coach and I grew up watching him coach the Lakers. How awesome would it be to return to the NBA and play for Coach Riley?

Well, that dream ended fast. The Heat worked me out and had me play in their summer camp, but then politely told me they weren't interested at that time. I was told no roster spot would be available but that I should keep in touch.

In the meantime, the NBA and Players' Association had another work stoppage. The league locked out the players, and it would lead to a cancellation of games until January 1999. For a while there was talk that the entire season would be lost.

This presented a real crossroads for me. What do I do next?

I had turned twenty-six years old in August of 1998. Twenty-six may not sound old, but athletes are seen as aging in dog years. In fact, in the NBA, twenty-six years old is the average player's age—the middle of one's career. And yet there I was, trying to get my career started up again and hoping to land a spot at the end of someone's bench. And I couldn't find any takers. At the same time, the league itself was in a labor crisis that endangered the season.

It was a bad mix of circumstances.

So, I said to myself, *All right, as opposed to wasting my time in NBA camps and summer leagues, trying to latch onto the last spot on a roster, I should go to Europe and embrace it.*

Put the NBA in the rearview window. Accept that I wasn't going back.

I didn't need the NBA to make a living playing basketball.

I didn't need the NBA to play the sport that I loved.

I loved the grind and the dedication that playing basketball required. That would keep me going for a long time. It honestly didn't matter where I played. I could play anywhere in the world. The only thing that mattered was that I played.

Feeling recharged, I then considered different opportunities to play in Europe. There were several, and I signed a one-year contract to play for Club Baloncesto Valladolid in Castile-Leon, Spain.

In Spain the O'Bannon family lived a really good life. While I wasn't making millions of dollars a year anymore, earning in the ballpark of $400,000 affords one plenty of comfort. Plus, the team pays for your housing, utilities, cable TV, and car. Many expenses are removed from the equation.

Our children were also young enough—they were two, four, and six when we moved to Europe—that relocating wouldn't be too disruptive. They weren't leaving behind many close friends or school activities or sports. And they were still dependent on Rosa and me.

The transition to Spain was also aided by the fact that Rosa is fluent in Spanish. Her language abilities helped us a lot while we lived in Spain, though we found that most Europeans spoke at least some English.

We lived it up. We often went out to dinner. With the European Union, our visa allowed us to travel throughout the continent. On my off days, we would hop onto the train to visit different countries. We saw the Vatican. We shopped in Rome. We rode on the gondolas in Venice. We did all the sightseeing one family could possibly do in Berlin and learned about all its history—and of course we'd occasionally swing by a McDonald's or Burger King to remind us of home!

Rosa, though, was the MVP of our family. She would pack everyone's bags and travel around the world with three little kids. She also homeschooled our children, all of whom would grow up to become star students. Rosa is really amazing.

In terms of my basketball career, while the competition in Europe wasn't quite as high as the NBA, it was significantly higher than either college or American minor leagues. European players were very skilled and many of them could have played in the NBA.

And for some Americans over there, they could become true stars. Legends, even.

Take Tyus Edney. As I mentioned earlier, Tyus and I had grown up playing in the same park—Victoria Park, right in Carson City—and of course we played together at UCLA. Our parents were also great friends. So basically we've known each other our whole lives.

Well, Tyus played for a few years in the NBA, for the Sacramento Kings and the Celtics, but then went on to become one of the best players in Europe from 1998 to 2009. He played in Lithuania, Italy, and Greece, and won various player of the year and all-star team awards along the way. I'm sure he earned over $1 million annually over there.

One day I was having a pregame meal with teammates in Barcelona at a sports bar, and on the TV was a game in which Tyus was playing. I'm talking to him through the TV, telling him how to do this and to do that. One of my teammates leans over and says to me, "Wait, you know Tyus Edney? *The* Tyus Edney?" He acted like I knew Michael Jordan or Kobe Bryant! Initially I thought he was kidding, but I soon realized he was being completely serious. "I've known him my whole life."

Every now and then I tell that story to Tyus—who's now back at UCLA as an assistant coach. Like me, he had a blast playing and living in Europe.

So instead of comparing a European basketball career to an NBA career, it's better to embrace it for what it is. It is its own creature. And it is a wonderful thing.

Interestingly, my time abroad gave me a different perspective on amateurism. The whole *amateur* concept and rules surrounding college players made little sense to my European teammates, many of whom had turned pro as young teenagers. Let me give you an example. When I was a twenty-eight-year-old player in Poland, I'd pick up a fourteen-year-old teammate and drive him to games and back home. He couldn't drive, but he earned pay for his play, and was free to sign endorsement deals—just like an American actor or musician of his age could. If this boy had been born in the United States he'd have to wait at least another five years before he could earn money for his labor and likeness. Talk about ridiculous. My European teammates thought amateurism was really odd.

But it was a great run abroad. Like the Ninth Circuit's holding, it wasn't exactly what I wanted. But it changed my life and, I think, made the world around me better too.

CHAPTER 14

CALL TO ACTION: MY TWELVE IDEAS FOR FIXING COLLEGE SPORTS

I'D LIKE TO THINK THAT I HELPED TO BRING SOME JUSTICE AND fairness to college sports. But I'm also a realist. I know that so much more needs to be done. So where do we go from here? I have a dozen ideas that I'll be promoting in the years ahead. I hope you join me in sharing them.

1.   Learning from Lonzo Ball and Donald De La Haye: Empower college athletes to capitalize on their brands.

I have never demanded that college athletes receive a salary or a wage. I also didn't spend a day in court advocating that college athletes be considered employees under the law. Further, no one can say that I have tried to convince college athletes to unionize. No doubt, those are all worthy and important topics. They should be debated and discussed. Their pros and cons should be weighed.

But they should also be kept separate from my line of thinking.

You see, what I have asked for doesn't require a revolution. I simply want college athletes to be able to control their names, likenesses, and images—in other words, to be able to control their brands. Just like other college students can do. Just like other athletes and entertainers can do. Just like, well, basically everyone except college athletes can do.

This is not a big ask nor an unreasonable wish. It's about basic fairness and common sense. It's also an idea that is already in place and one on which the NCAA appears to be coming around.

Take LaVar Ball. You probably know him as dad to three Los Angeles basketball phenoms: Los Angeles Lakers guard Lonzo Ball, former UCLA guard LiAngelo Ball, and former Chino Hills High School guard LaMelo Ball. Yes, LaVar is outspoken and sometimes goes too far. Let's get that out of the way. He occasionally says things that make me cringe. It's one thing to be bold. It's another to be bombastic. But don't be distracted by Ball's bluster and swagger. The man also understands sports business and how to work around ill-advised rules.

This is apparent in Ball's "Big Baller Brand." I don't know if I love BBB's designs, but I sure love how Lonzo wore BBB apparel throughout his time at UCLA. You would see him wear BBB during Bruins practices, on TV interviews, and in YouTube spots. BBB shirts. BBB hats. BBB socks. You name it. B. B. B.

Meanwhile, LaVar's website would sell those same items on the family's website, which featured the three Ball sons. There were even blue-and-gold items for sale that sure looked like they were inspired by Lonzo's connection to UCLA.

Lonzo wore the BBB brand confidently and without hesi-tation—and, most importantly, in spite of the NCAA. You see, the NCAA prohibits college athletes from using their names or images to promote the sale of commercial products and services. It's hard to conclude how Lonzo wasn't breaking that rule, if not technically then at least in spirit.

What did the NCAA do about it? Absolutely nothing.

Sure, the NCAA pressured UCLA to in turn pressure LaVar to remove his son from BBB promotions and website videos, but LaVar would have none of it. He kept on trucking.

Did Lonzo lose his eligibility? Nope. The NCAA looked the other way.

More recently, LiAngelo Ball was at UCLA until his father pulled him from school in the aftermath of a shoplifting incident in China. Though LiAngelo's not—at least not yet—a superstar like his older brother, he still hawked BBB apparel without fear. The same goes for little brother LaMelo, who, as a high school athlete through 2017, already had his own signature shoe through BBB. Their father doesn't seem all that worried about the NCAA and amateurism. LaVar has rejected every request or demand that he stop generating money for his family through his sons' identities. By December 2017, LaVar decided "enough was enough" and arranged for LiAngleo and LeMelo to turn pro by signing with Vytautas Prienai-Birštonas of the Lithuanian Basketball League.

Just say no. Sometimes that is all you need to do.

Given the Ball experience, I'd like to think the NCAA maybe realizes that the tide is turning. Even if the NCAA won't admit it, it might have finally seen the light: college athletes should be able to control their brand because it is *their own* brand.

It's not difficult or far-fetched to envision other college athletes being able to market their brands. And one needn't be an NBA lottery pick or NFL first-round pick to benefit.

Enter Donald De La Haye. Until the summer of 2017 De La Haye was a kicker for the University of Central Florida Knights. He still attends UCF, though no longer on an athletic scholarship.

Let me explain why.

De La Haye has become famous not because of his kicking, but because of his YouTube channel, "Deestroying," which has over 150,000 subscribers and has been viewed more than five million times. In addition to being athletic, the man knows how to make some great videos! Some of De La Haye's YouTube clips are about kicking, and they're creatively done. Others feature De La Haye shooting basketballs and running. And still others consist of pranks on his friends. He's a charismatic young man who I'm certain has a future in Hollywood.

My favorite video, though, is where De La Haye hilariously trolls the NCAA in a parody of an ESPN "This is *SportsCenter*" commercial. In it, he's sitting in an office and on the phone, pretending to work for the NCAA. "How much are we getting out of it?" De La Haye asks the person on the other line. "Nothing?! Shut him down, shut him down, shut him down, no questions asked!"

The young man is a blast.

And, yes, De La Haye is making money from his brand. YouTube allows users to enable monetization and De La Haye has exercised that option. Although the amount of YouTube money earned varies based on how many people watch an accompanying ad and other factors, I hear the typical pay to a well-known YouTube user is about twenty dollars per one thousand views. So, De La Haye may have already earned somewhere in the ballpark of $100,000 on his YouTube videos. YouTube hasn't made De La Haye rich, but it has allowed him to benefit from his brand, just like his school and the NCAA have done.

Even though the NCAA avoided conflict with Lonzo Ball, it decided to take on De La Haye. Maybe it was afraid of the Ball family but not afraid of a lesser-known kid who's "only" a kicker. I'm not sure. In any event, in August 2017, the NCAA told De La Haye that he had to stop profiting from videos that are "athletics-related," whatever that means (talk about creating a vague standard!). The NCAA also ordered him to move his existing "athletics-related" videos into a nonmonetized account. If De La Haye didn't do these things, the NCAA warned, he would lose his NCAA eligibility.

Basically, the NCAA demanded De La Haye abandon control of his brand. De La Haye did the right thing: he said no.

Although UCF has suspended De La Haye from the football team, he's now making more videos with more subscribers and views than ever before. I'd like to think he's generating more revenue than the value of his scholarship. Even if he isn't, he's taken a stand for what's right.

I hope other college athletes take direction from De La Haye. Sure, they may not be as captivating and engaging as he is. But this is really about principle. If you craft a brand, it is your brand to control.

Now, I realize NCAA officials have long insisted that if college athletes were in any way compensated, college sports would lose fans. They argued this theory in my trial. The fact is, that is not true. UCLA didn't lose one fan because Lonzo Ball wore BBB apparel. And how many UCF football fans were lost because De La Haye masterminded YouTube content that sometimes dealt with his football career? The answer is none. If anything, Ball and De La Haye generated publicity for UCLA and UCF, respectively, through their brand management. They probably attracted new fans to those programs as a result.

The NCAA has also insisted that college athletes marketing their names, images, and likenesses would somehow harm their studies.

False—yet again.

In fact, if the NCAA truly cared about education and graduation rates, it would let its athletes control, develop, and capitalize on their brands. Some players would be more inclined to stay in college and further their education. Plus, games would then have more experienced players who are more polished, which would be a more attractive product for college fans.

I also think college athlete brand management is essential because of the widespread perception that star college players are taking money under the table. A not-uncommon belief exists that agents and hustlers are handing star players wads of cash in order to gain their association and friendship. There's a stigma that goes along with this perception. People view the players as unethical, even criminal. That stigma is especially concerning since the vast majority of players believed to be taking payments are black.

Now, I'm not naïve. Letting athletes control their brand wouldn't eliminate this perception and it wouldn't necessarily deter athletes from taking money.

But it might for some.

If athletes are able to control and profit from their brands, the payments to the star athletes could prove substantial. And these payments would be conducted "over the table." There would be licensing contracts and endorsement deals. They would be subject to taxes and everything else that makes a transaction "legitimate" in the eyes of the law.

As I mentioned above, athlete control of the brand isn't just for star basketball and football players. I realize many of the top beneficiaries would be those players, but college sports isn't just about men's hoops and football. There are many women soccer players, hockey players, swimmers, softball players, and other college athletes—male and female—who could possess advertising appeal based on their unique skills and identities. They could control their brands and license them to apparel, equipment, and sporting goods companies, among others in the sports world.

And I'm not just talking about Division I college athletes, either. I get that they are the most likely to be on television and to attract the notice of ESPN. But many Division III schools are popular in their surrounding communities, and so too are their athletes.

I recognize that these ideas might scare some who work at the NCAA. Then again, the NCAA has already adopted them, at least in part, with respect to Olympic athletes.

When an American athlete wins a medal at the Olympics, he or she also receives a payment from the US Olympic Committee (USOC). This is through the USOC's Operation Gold program, which pays $37,500 to gold medalists, $22,500 to silver medalists, and $15,000 to bronze medalists. Operation Gold also pays American athletes who win medals in other competitions, including the World Championships. Other countries have similar programs. Basically, these programs ensure that these incredible, truly extraordinary athletes receive a bit more than only the medals that are presented to them.

Shouldn't those monetary awards prevent Olympic athletes from participating in NCAA sports? After all, these athletes have earned money from their unique abilities and identities. And, as we know through Donald De La Haye's experience, NCAA rules instruct that an athlete forfeits his or her eligibility upon receiving "any payment" that is in any conceivable way based on athletic performance. Yet many Olympians are college athletes. Many others later become college athletes.

Take Katie Ledecky. She is a five-time Olympic gold medalist and fourteen-time world champion. She now swims for Stanford University with her NCAA eligibility intact. That is how it should work. The NCAA shouldn't hold Katie's success against her. Unfortunately for Katie, though, she still can't accept endorsement deals, at least not if she wants to continue swimming at Stanford. The NCAA is reasonable only to a point.

So what, exactly, is the NCAA protecting? Is it worried that it wouldn't be able to compete with the athletes themselves over who can best utilize their brand? That's not about education. That's about self-preservation.

The bottom line is that college athletes should be able to take advantage of their brands while that brand is marketable.

Besides, if doing so causes those athletes to become distracted from their studies or from their team commitments, remember that there are already mechanisms in place that would kick in. You get bad grades? You get thrown out of school. You show up late to practice? You get benched. You show up to practice late again? You get tossed from the team. This isn't rocket science here. Brand control and transparency would improve college sports. And it would do wonders for many young men and women as well as their sports.

Brand control and transparency also relate to the late 2017 federal criminal charges that have been brought against sneaker executives and coaches.

Imagine if the NCAA had tried to settle my lawsuit. The NCAA could have done so simply by changing its rules to let athletes market their own brands. That approach would have opened up new doors for high school kids to take social media by storm. Some of these kids are super-creative, too, or at least have access to folks who fit that bill. Players would have been able to market themselves for financial gain and do so in a world where payments are recorded and transactions are transparent. I'd like to think that in this kind of a world—a world where the NCAA voluntarily made the changes I sought—some of these bribes wouldn't have occurred and the Justice Department wouldn't now be involved. Some of the kids, or at least their parents, would have defiantly said, "No, thanks," when tempted by shoe company peddlers holding bags full of hundred-dollar bills. These kids and their families wouldn't have needed that kind of dirty money. They could earn it on their own, and the money would be clean.

Now, I realize that there are greedy people, and some people will always ask for more no matter how much they get. But I also know that most people play by the rules, especially when those rules are fair and sensible.

Empower the talent to earn what is rightfully theirs and watch corruption go way down.

As a final point, if the NCAA doesn't change on the issue of athlete control of brand, others might try to take its place. Andy Schwartz, who was retained as an economist in my case, hopes to convince historically black colleges and universities to exit the NCAA and form their own league. In it, the athletes would control their brand and be paid a salary. Whether or not Andy's idea works out, it highlights that things don't have to stay the same. If the twenty-first century has taught us anything, it's about the power of ideas and technologies to disrupt the status quo and reshape entire industries. Uber. Wikipedia. Smartphones. Perhaps NCAA leaders feel comfortable at the moment, but innovation is always lurking.

2. Empower college athletes to participate in NCAA rulemaking, interpretation, and enforcement.

In what system does a person impacted by a rulemaking body have no say over the rules?

I know there are other countries where that happens. We've fought wars against some of them. We've given up lives to ensure that fascism and other harmful ideologies didn't take over our way of life.

That's because in the United States we have the right to vote out lawmakers with whom we disagree. And when a federal administrative agency takes a hostile action against us, we can appeal it through the courts.

Then we have the NCAA. The NCAA frequently adopts, interprets, and enforces rules that restrict the livelihoods of college athletes. Yet those athletes have no meaningful say at any level of the process.

College athletes are largely shut out from how NCAA amateurism rules are created, interpreted, and enforced. This is a very different setup from the ones experienced by professional athletes and Olympic athletes, both of whom are provided with real power over how rules are shaped and, through arbitration, legitimate forums to resolve disputes.

None of that happens for college athletes.

That must change. College athletes should be viewed as partners in college sports, not as dependents or subjects of the NCAA.

The NCAA should already know this. The criminal prosecutions of sneaker executives and college coaches show how corrupt the game has become. If the NCAA had been listening to players, those players would have had stories to share about being offered bags of cash. Instead, the NCAA put on earmuffs and blindfolds.

Hear no evil. See no evil.

Now, I realize the NCAA adopted a system in the late '90s that is supposed to provide college athletes with a voice. Student-athlete advisory committees, or SAACs, are college athlete committees found on college campuses across the country. Each is composed of a representative from each sports team at a school. Each SAAC then nominates a representative to be part of a conference SAAC, which then nominates a representative to be part of a national SAAC.

Don't get me wrong—SAACs are better than nothing. I wish they had existed when I played. I would have tried to become the UCLA men's basketball team representative.

But nowhere in any NCAA rule or bylaw is it stated that SAACs have power to make any changes.

From what I have learned about SAACs, they only act as

advisory bodies or focus groups. They have no actual authority. They don't vote on the creation or interpretation of rules. They don't play a role in how those rules are enforced. SAACs do offer college athletes a chance to react and comment, albeit indirectly, on NCAA legislation. But there is no procedure for SAACs to actually strike down such legislation, formally construct their own proposed legislation, or challenge established NCAA bylaws. And if a college athlete gets in trouble with the NCAA, SAACs play no role whatsoever in whether the athlete is punished and in whether the athlete can wage an effective appeal.

So, SAACs may make college athletes feel involved, but they don't make them actually involved.

That is simply not good enough. College athletes shouldn't be window-dressing when there are real problems behind those windows. Those athletes should have a true vote on NCAA rules, both in the creation of those rules and in how they are interpreted and enforced. Having a "voice" isn't enough. Voices can be tuned out. Voices can be ignored. Voices can be forgotten.

Votes count. Votes matter. Votes last.

If the NCAA wants to hold onto power, it's got to learn to empower those who give the NCAA a reason to exist.

3. Make NCAA rules and forms understandable to college athletes and their families, and involve athletes and their families in choice of words.

Let me start by paying the NCAA a compliment—and I realize that compliments to the NCAA have been few and far between in this book. I appreciate the NCAA making its numerous rules available for free. Those rules can be downloaded without cost at the NCAA's website. Rosa and I have downloaded them on several occasions. We did so not for my case against the NCAA but because our children are, or were, NCAA athletes and we had questions about their respective rights.

Thanks, NCAA, for not hiding the ball. Transparency is worth at least two points on my scoring sheet.

That's the good news. The bad news: NCAA rules are written in what at times seems like a foreign language. Those rules are incredibly complex and unwelcoming, almost as if one needs a PhD in NCAA Studies to understand them.

Let me explain. NCAA rules are spread out single-spaced over 32 articles that are found in a 430-page PDF document titled "NCAA Division I Manual: Constitution, Operating Bylaws, Administrative Bylaws."

Nothing says, "Read me," like a 430-page PDF file, single-spaced! The lack of spacing would be more manageable if NCAA rules were worded like normal people speak and write. Instead, NCAA bylaws are often written in convoluted language. Try these two rules out:

> 14.2.1.1.1 Prohibited Practice Activities. A prospective student-athlete shall not engage in any practice activities (e.g., review of playbook, chalk talk, film review) with a coaching staff member prior to his or her enrollment. A prospective student-athlete who has signed a National Letter of Intent or the institution's written offer of admission and/or financial aid, or has submitted a financial deposit to the institution in response to the institution's offer of admission shall not observe an institution's off-field or off-court practice session (e.g., meeting, film review) that is closed to the general public. A prospective student-athlete may observe an institution's on-field or on-court practice session (including a session that is closed to the general public), regardless of whether he or she has signed a National Letter of Intent or the institution's written offer of admission and/or financial

aid, or has submitted a financial deposit to the institution in response to the institution's offer of admission.

17.18.5.1.1.1 Competition That Exceeds Two Days. An institution that participates in multiple competitions on the same date that it participates in a competition that exceeds two days may select either day (but not both days) as one institutional date of competition. Further, if the institution participates in a separate event on the selected date, such participation will not result in an additional date of competition. However, participation in a separate event at a separate site on the date not selected will result in a second date of competition if the institution has the minimum number of student-athletes participating on that day.

Remember, these are seventeen-, eighteen-, and nineteen-year-olds—teenagers—who are among those regulated by these rules and who need to understand them to fully understand their rights and obligations. Would you have been able to understand that verbiage as a teenager? If not, would someone who is neutral and whom you trust be available to help you do so?

You might almost wonder if these rules are worded to confuse people. Or maybe they are designed to discourage students and parents from reading further and learning about their potential rights. That would be a terrible thing, since these rights are really important and impactful. But if the rights-holders don't understand their rights, those rights become a lot less valuable.

Along those lines, to expect students or families—even educated ones who have sports backgrounds—to understand NCAA language is unrealistic.

And it's not just students and their families, either.

I've talked with many coaches about NCAA rules. Granted, coaches' attitudes about rules aren't necessarily the "correct" ones, at least from the standpoint of students and parents. After all, coaches' interests don't always align with those of players and parents. But even assuming everyone's interests were aligned, coaches—like students and parents—often don't understand NCAA rules. So how can they possibly advise students on rules they themselves don't understand? In reality, when students, parents, and coaches discuss rules they are often all confused or mistaken.

And it's not just the NCAA rulebook, either. There are numerous forms that a college athlete must sign upon starting his or her collegiate career.

Take the Free Application for Federal Student Aid (FAFSA), which my own children have signed. Rosa and I have talked to other parents of college athletes about it. Given that both of us are college grads and are already familiar with college sports—not to mention that Rosa works in education—we're advantaged when it comes to trying to grasp the FAFSA process. Many of our friends whose children play college sports are not. FAFSA is a sore topic with them.

Now, normally a school's athletic department tells the student that he or she needs to complete the FAFSA form in order to receive the athletic scholarship.

That's fine.

The problem is that many students and their parents believe that completing the FAFSA form means a loan has been taken out. It hasn't.

The confusion is worsened by the fact that completing a FAFSA requires parents' full disclosure of tax returns. This tax requirement delays and sometimes interferes with students receiving the full cost of attendance. It can also cause students to get charged late fees and be dropped from classes.

If a college athlete is receiving both an academic scholarship and an athletic scholarship, the paperwork only gets more cumbersome. This process is confusing and deceptive—and needs to be fixed.

I get that NCAA rules and FAFSA might not be purposefully confusing, but it's not a stretch to assume that the NCAA has little motivation to fix processes that help to cover up what more seasoned observers of college sports can see is a potentially deceptive system.

So where is the NCAA on this problem? Well, the NCAA tries to address it through a system of "compliance officers." Colleges' athletic departments employ them. Their job is to make sure their school, coaches, staff, and players are complying with NCAA rules.

It is far from an ideal system. For starters, compliance officers tend to be lawyers. That's not a bad thing per se, but it highlights the high level of critical reading and analysis necessary to be "fluent" in NCAA bylaws. Many compliance officers, in fact, spend much of their time answering questions and interpreting bylaws for confused coaches and athletes. Often the compliance officers can be found teaching coaches about NCAA rules because the rules are too confusing.

Second, athletes learning from compliance officers about NCAA rules doesn't provide those athletes with a neutral "translator" of the NCAA's language. Compliance officers work for the schools, not the players. To the extent there is an actual or possible conflict between a school and a player, the compliance officer is obligated to take the side of the school. It's like negotiating a contract with a business in another country and letting the foreign business take care of all the interpretations. You would never do that. Just like I always hired someone to translate and review any contracts to play in a foreign country—I wasn't going to rely on what the team told me.

Now, the NCAA might argue that its rules need to be complex because the business of college sports is so complex. That may be true, but ask yourself, "Why is that the case?" And how can the NCAA plead complexity on one hand while preaching the simple, bright-line gospel of amateurism on the other?

NCAA rules should be rewritten as part of a collaborative process that involves not just NCAA executives and lawyers but also coaches, athletes, and families of athletes. Please use plain-spoken language. Please value clarity. Don't try to head-fake the reader.

If this means forming a commission to rewrite NCAA rules then so be it. But make sure *all* of the stakeholders have a spot on that committee.

It is clear that the language in the NCAA bylaws is simply not user-friendly for student-athletes, families, and coaches. There would be a widespread benefit to clarifying and streamlining these rules.

4. Allow college athletes to transfer colleges without a penalty.

Choosing a college is a life-altering decision for any teenager. There are so many factors to consider. The dollar amount of available scholarships and financial aid is often critical. Academic programs, culture, nightlife, and location are also important. Not all of these factors are easy to quantify and weigh. Plus, there are so many unknowns, like whether a student will actually fit in with their classmates or whether the programs are as good as advertised.

Judging a school based on how much one enjoys admitted students weekend is risky—just like picking a college sports program after a visit with the coach and players. There's just a lot you don't know.

While most students stick by their choice of college, some, after a year or two, realize that the school isn't right for them.

Thankfully, they aren't necessarily stuck. They can seek to transfer. All it takes is sending out transfer applications to other colleges. If accepted, the student can leave their current school and enroll in the new one. It's pretty simple and happens quite often.

This should go without saying, but the student doesn't need to notify their current college or gets its permission in order to transfer. That would be strange, right? If you want to switch colleges, you should be able to. It's not like you signed a noncompete clause to attend a college. It's a school, not an employer…right?

Once the transfer has occurred, the student can take classes at the new school in the first available semester. The march toward graduation isn't interrupted. After all, it wouldn't make much sense if the transfer student had to wait a semester or two in order to take classes. In fact, if that were the case, many unhappy students might not even consider the transfer option. Those students would be stuck in a place where they don't want to be.

Let's now talk about college *athletes* who wish to transfer. In short, the system tells them, "Don't!"

Transfer rules for college athletes are completely different with respect to athletic participation. For starters, the athlete needs to first obtain permission from his or her current school just to *contact* other schools. Why is that? Because the current school must agree to release the athlete from the athletic scholarship or he or she won't be able to receive an athletic scholarship at the new school.

Imagine being that athlete. You have to ask in order to leave, but what happens if the answer is no or the transfer attempt doesn't materialize? Or how about worrying about how your coach will react? You might be viewed as a traitor, or at least become the source of resentment from the coaching staff. This step alone imposes a cost on an athlete: once the transfer request is made, there's really no going back.

Some college coaches have used athletes' transfer requests

against those athletes. For selfish competition reasons that have nothing to do with education, the coach can effectively block the athlete from transferring to some schools but not others.

Even if the transfer is approved, another cost appears. Per NCAA rules, when a college athlete transfers to a new college, the athlete must sit out one full season of competition. Sure, that student can watch games from the sidelines and even practice with the team.

But play? No go.

Now, the college losing the player can waive the sit-out rule, but usually they don't, especially when the transfer is intraconference. The bottom line is that colleges want to discourage college athletes from changing schools—even though college coaches, college athletic directors, and college athletic staff do it all the time, without penalty.

To treat athletes differently from other students contradicts the NCAA's decree that "these are all just college students." The NCAA should do the right thing and allow athletic transfers to occur in the same way academic transfers occur.

5. Make college athletes' amateurism rights the same regardless of which sport they play.

Throughout this book I have discussed amateurism mainly as it relates to college basketball and college football. That's because I'm most familiar with those two college sports and also because they generate the bulk of the revenue that makes the business of college sports work so nicely for the NCAA, conferences, and schools.

The NCAA, however, preaches that we shouldn't concern ourselves with things like revenue and profits from any sport. From their pulpit, the focus of NCAA analysis should be on college athletes' education and ensuring that these students are treated equally.

That's fine by me. College athletes should be treated equally. And so you'd expect that *amateurism* would mean the same thing for all college athletes, regardless of their sport, right? Well, as is often the case with the NCAA, making assumptions—even logical ones—can get you into a lot of trouble.

As a starting point, consider what happens to college basketball and football underclassmen when an agent represents them in any kind of communication with a pro team: they lose their NCAA eligibility. Now consider what happens when these underclassmen participate in the NBA and NFL drafts: once again, they lose their NCAA eligibility.

This is true even if they aren't drafted. And quite a few of them won't be drafted. In fact, according to the NFL, nearly one-third of underclassmen don't get their names called. The numbers are similar in the NBA. For the 2017 NBA draft, 137 underclassmen declared. Yet only sixty players are taken in the two-round NBA draft, and those players include college seniors, underclassmen, and international pros.

So where do all these undrafted underclassmen go? Going back to college often isn't a realistic option since their athletic scholarships have been given to other players. If they do return to school, they can't play their sport and they'll have to foot the bill of tuition, room, board, and books.

These players can try to hook on to an American minor league or, at least in the case of basketball, go play abroad and earn a wage. But as I mentioned earlier, American minor leagues don't play especially well. Plus, roster spots on foreign teams are limited in various ways.

So again, where do they go? The reality is, many of these players try to find other kinds of jobs, without the benefit of a college degree. Many struggle to find employment.

This system is far from ideal.

The same is not at all true for college hockey players. They benefit from a completely different set of NCAA rules that ensure that the NHL draft is much less of a make-or-break life experience.

NHL teams can draft hockey players when they are eighteen years old. The drafted player and his NHL team then have a candid discussion about his future. Most drafted players aren't yet ready for the NHL, so they typically elect to play in either junior hockey or college hockey on an athletic scholarship.

Let me stress that point for a moment.

The drafted hockey player can attend college, and do so on a full athletic scholarship. The fact that he was drafted and had discussions with NHL teams is not held against him in any way.

He can then play NCAA hockey until he graduates or signs with an NHL team, which controls his rights for five years. The player can develop in college, both in terms of his hockey skills and as a person. He and the NHL team that drafted him can continually assess when the ideal time for him to make the jump would be. The player's development and the team's needs are all part of the conversation. This approach makes it less likely a player will leave college too early and fail.

Even better for college hockey players, they can get advice from so-called advisors, who—it just so happens—are often agents. The advisors can counsel a player on the best time to turn pro. No, the advisor can't pay or be paid, nor can he or she be in contact with NHL teams. But the advisor can be extremely helpful to a college hockey player.

Meanwhile, if a hockey player isn't drafted, he can later sign with an NHL team. Plenty have done so and some have become NHL stars, like Adam Oates and Martin St. Louis.

This is a very smart system. The college player and his NHL team can have a continuing conversation about when and if it would make sense to turn pro before the end of college. And the player receives advice from people who are genuinely knowledgeable. So the divide between "amateur" and "pro" is made gradually, on a continuum, rather than at a blunt, irreversible moment.

So why are college hockey players treated so differently? It's because of competition. The NCAA faces legitimate competition from the Canadian Hockey League for college-age hockey players. The CHL governs roughly sixty "junior" hockey teams that are part of the Ontario Hockey League, the Quebec Major Junior Hockey League or the Western Hockey League. Because of the CHL, the NCAA must offer relaxed restrictions or it would lose players.

As it stands now, the choice between NCAA and CHL hockey is one filled with pros and cons. A player in junior hockey can end up playing a schedule similar to one in the NHL. Between preseason, regular season, and postseason, he can play in close to a hundred games. In contrast, a college hockey player tends to play in only about forty games. CHL players are also paid, albeit not much—about $400 a week. NCAA players receive college educations, though with all of the time constraints discussed earlier in this book. The CHL is a primary source of NHL players. A little more than 50 percent of NHL players come from the CHL, while about 30 percent are from the college ranks. Only 60 of the 217 players selected in the 2017 NHL draft were NCAA players or recruits.

The larger point is that there is a choice for hockey players, with each possibility having pros and cons. Because there is a choice, the NCAA can't be as severe in how it treats hockey players. Simply put, the NHL has less leverage when it comes to hockey because substitutes exist.

And it isn't just college hockey players who experience a different system of "amateurism." College baseball players do as well. I'm very familiar with this, as our son, Edward III, is a left-handed pitcher for the University of Pacific Tigers. He and his teammates encounter the baseball version of amateurism.

Here's how it works with baseball players. Under Major League Baseball rules, a player can be drafted by a big-league team right out of high school and then enter a minor league system. He doesn't have to sign, however. He can instead go to college, hope to improve his game there, and then be eligible to be drafted again while in college. If he attends a four-year college, he'll be eligible as a junior; if he attends a junior college, it's only a one-year commitment. These aren't NCAA rules—these are MLB rules.

But the NCAA plays a role because it permits an "advisor" to help a drafted baseball player decide when to turn pro. And when the NCAA has tried to impose limits on the advice offered by an advisor, courts have stepped in. About eight years ago, the NCAA paid Oklahoma State pitcher Andy Oliver $750,000 to settle a lawsuit Oliver had filed after the NCAA forced his school to suspend him because his advisor may have talked with the Minnesota Twins, the team that drafted him out of high school. The judge in that case ordered the NCAA not to enforce its no-agent rule because to do so was completely unfair to Oliver and other drafted players.

Here's what the NCAA should do: (1) allow *all* college athletes to go through professional drafts and, whether or not they are drafted, let them return to college; and (2) allow *all* college athletes to get advice from anyone they like, including sports agents.

The fact is, allowing players to be drafted and still return to college sports if they decline to sign is a model that has worked well for the NHL. The player can leave college when he has enough polish, life experience, and maturity. The NCAA would probably benefit, too. More players would decide to remain in college. Maybe there would be fewer "one-and-done" players in basketball. That would be a good thing for everyone.

Besides, shouldn't the NCAA praise young players who seek out the most information possible in order to make an informed choice about turning pro? In life and school, those who do their homework are typically those whom we admire. A young player discussing his pro prospects with an agent, who can in turn speak with team executives about that player's pro readiness, should be encouraged, not viewed with suspicion.

You would think that ensuring that a college athlete is truly ready for the pros and not abandoning education too early would be a more important goal for the NCAA than upholding an invented definition of "amateurism."

You would think.

Now, you might be saying to yourself, "Wait a second, Ed. Agents are bad people and they would exploit college athletes if given the chance." Listen, are there bad agents? Sure, just like there are some bad teachers and bad plumbers and bad every kind of worker.

But, similarly to those professions, agents don't operate in a vacuum. They are licensed and held accountable. In fact, sports agents representing players in the major sports leagues are tightly regulated. That's because pro players' associations impose ethical and legal duties on them in order for them to have a license to represent. There are also state laws that play a role.

The bottom line is that agents typically aren't bandits and crooks. I get that that is how they are caricatured, but real life is different. And if they break the law or break a rule, they are held accountable. Let's not be afraid of the boogeyman here—most agents do a good job and are very knowledgeable.

As a final point, it's hard to ignore race in this discussion. A system in which basketball and football players are treated differently from hockey and baseball players raises questions about why certain groups are treated differently. You could argue that it seems discriminatory, if not in intent then in effect. The fact is, most Division I college basketball and college football players are black, and that is not true of Division I college hockey and college baseball players.

Like I mentioned earlier in this book, deliberate attempts to hurt black people consist of only the far end of a long spectrum of racism. Simply not seeing race as a factor is much more common and also problematic.

For all these reasons, it would make a lot of sense for the NCAA to equalize treatment of college athletes.

6. Guarantee health benefits for college athletes.

College athletes are just like anyone else who plays a sport: at risk of injury. My knee knows that all too well. So what happens when a college athlete is injured? The good news is that the athlete will almost certainly have insurance. That's because insurance is an NCAA requirement for eligibility.

Unfortunately for the athlete, universities aren't required to pay for that insurance. Worse yet, college athletes can lose their athletic scholarships after suffering an injury.

In both obvious and subtle ways, this landscape presents major financial risks for athletes and their families.

The obvious risks can be found in the health of those who play football and other sports where head injuries are common. Every month, it seems, there's a new scientific finding about neurological health and playing contact sports.

And the finding is always bad.

Chronic traumatic encephalopathy, or CTE, has been detected in over 90 percent of brains of deceased NFL and college football players who agreed to partake in studies. These players are also much more likely to suffer other neurological problems as they age.

It's all very dispiriting. I know contact sports players who over the years have seen their health erode. I realize they to some degree knew what they were getting into, but I don't think they—or their parents—were warned about the severity of the risks.

And it's hard to imagine things getting much better. Now, I take hope in the fact that some of our smartest researchers are devoted to making contact sports safer, but the reality is that these kinds of sports probably can't be made "safe." Each year athletes are stronger, heavier, and faster than those who played before. The contact is getting more impactful, not less.

This is probably why Dr. Bennet Omalu—the doctor whom Will Smith played in the movie *Concussion*—recently said that it is "child abuse" for children to play football. He recommended that no one under the age of eighteen play football, ice hockey, mixed martial arts, boxing, rugby, or wrestling. I'm not sure I would go as far as Dr. Omalu, but I am very worried about the future health of the young men and women who play these sports.

Worse yet, the young men and women who go on to play contact sports in college do so at their own peril. Neither the NCAA nor any college is required to offer healthcare to college athletes while they are in school or during the decades of life that follow.

Look, most of these players will never play in the NFL or become rich. But many of them will develop serious neurological problems as they age. Whether they have the money to pay to treat those problems is unknown. Given that affordable healthcare in the United States is a reach for a lot of people—to put it kindly—there's a real risk of suffering, both for former players and their families.

Remember, these players gave everything they had to their

schools. They made them a lot of money, too. They made students more likely to apply. They made alumni more likely to donate.

Don't the schools have a moral obligation to help them?

Lack of healthcare is also a problem when a student-athlete's insurance is out-of-network. In many cases, the athlete gets insurance through his or her parents. And, in many cases, the parents live in another part of the country.

This has been an issue with our kids playing sports out-of-state where our insurance didn't extend. Rosa and I have paid quite a bit of money when our children had sports-related health needs. It is yet another cost of being a college athlete that parents end up paying.

The fact that athletic scholarships aren't guaranteed only adds to the risk of playing college sports. Although the NCAA has permitted schools to offer multiyear athletic scholarships since 2012, multiyear scholarships remain fairly uncommon. Most schools continue to guarantee athletic scholarships on a year-to-year basis. Not surprisingly, a number of athletes have lost those scholarships after suffering injuries. Sure, they don't lose their spot as a student at that college, but now they have to find another way to pay for it. That just isn't right.

On a brighter note, I'm encouraged to see some states aren't staying on the sidelines when it comes to college player health.

In Connecticut, for example, state legislators are considering a bill that would make Connecticut the first state to regulate the NCAA's health practices. The proposed "athletic protection commission" would require best practices for injury and abuse reporting. School, conference, and NCAA staff would all become mandated reporting officers—meaning they would have no choice but to report injuries and abuse. The commission would also investigate complaints, protect whistleblowers, and punish institutions and individuals who don't follow the rules. In short, the Connecticut bill would add teeth to a bite that needs it. I like it.

The National College Players Association (NCPA) is also doing good work in this space. The NCPA advocates for college athletes in hopes of establishing mandatory health and safety standards. This organization highlights how college coaches have repeatedly returned concussed players to football games without any threat of discipline or even investigation by the NCAA.

How many more times do we have to see a player get banged in the head and keep playing?

I remember a few years back when the media—including CBS Sports and *Time* magazine—reported how University of Michigan coach Brady Hoke sent his quarterback, Shane Morris, back into a game after a vicious hit to the head. Morris was looking wobbly and stumbling all over the field (physicians later confirmed he had a concussion). But Hoke wanted to win. The university later apologized to Morris. The NCAA? It said that it had "full confidence" that Michigan would correct its mistakes without NCAA intervention.

Now keep in mind, this was a nationally televised game between two big-time college programs, the University of Michigan Wolverines and the University of Minnesota Golden Gophers. If it had involved smaller programs, would there even have been fallout? I don't know, but I do know these are young persons' lives at stake.

So as the NCPA stresses, why is it that the NCAA conducts massive investigations over college athletes who may have received money for signing autographs and who may lose their NCAA eligibility as a result and yet takes such little action in situations like the one involving Hoke and Morris?

The NCAA sure has some strange priorities. It's almost as if the NCAA cares more about "amateurism" and its effect on the bottom line than about the health of college athletes.

I realize healthcare is a complicated topic. I also know that when someone gets sick, providing healthcare becomes a much more expensive proposition than a lot of people would like to believe.

But colleges make the situation worse by not having to provide basic benefits to injured players.

This must change.

If universities are going to profit from athletics, they should treat the athletes fairly. Guaranteed healthcare should be provided at least while the college athlete attends college and hopefully there can be benefits for those athletes in the years that follow.

7. Guarantee the same freedom of expression for college athletes as exists for other college students.

College athletes should be able to express themselves. That doesn't mean being able to engage in hate speech or online bullying, but college athletes should enjoy the same latitude as their classmates. The same regarding what they say. The same regarding how they act. And the same regarding what they write, whether it be in term papers or on Snapchat. College athletes shouldn't have to worry about retaliation from a coach or a school.

For now, at least, those worries are real.

A number of college athletic programs have forbidden players from tweeting during the season. A number of those schools, including the University of Iowa and the University of Louisville, are public universities, where one would expect freedom of speech to be protected. That is just not the case.

At other schools, players are allowed to tweet but punished if their tweet causes controversy. Take what happened to Cardale Jones back in 2012. At the time, he was a quarterback for Ohio State, another public university. He tweeted, "Why should we have to go to class if we came here to play FOOTBALL, we ain't come to play SCHOOL classes are pointless."

In response, Ohio State and its coach, Urban Meyer, suspended Jones for one game.

Now, let me be clear about something: I don't like when a college athlete expresses that "classes are pointless." Education is always a positive. While I don't want to toot my own horn, I take great pride in the fact that I returned to UCLA to finish my degree. And in truth, the older you get, the more you realize those classes from college developed your brain and helped to make you the person you became. I'd like to think that, now years later, Jones sees that.

But that's not really the point here. The point is that if an Ohio State classmate of Jones had tweeted the exact same statement, he or she wouldn't have faced any discipline from the school. The First Amendment would have protected a tweet like that.

So, yeah, if a college athlete wants to use social media to advocate NCAA reform, he or she should have the right to do so—even if the language might make you cringe.

Same goes if a college athlete wants to take direction from their sports heroes and take a controversial stand, so be it. You want to sit, or raise your fist, during the National Anthem as a way of peacefully protesting social injustice? Then do it.

Why? Because this is America, where freedom of expression, even of views that are unpopular or that make people uncomfortable, are protected.

I actually think limiting athletes' speech exposes the NCAA as hypocritical.

On one hand, the NCAA and schools negotiate merchandise and sponsorship deals that prominently feature logos and student images. On the other, college athletes can't express personal views on armbands or tweet critical views. It doesn't seem right that colleges enjoy wide freedom of expression while athletes must follow strict parameters and not ever get out of line.

To be clear, with freedom comes responsibility. Like other

college students, college athletes can face repercussions for their social media posts that go too far. I know coaches look into recruits' social media pages. They might see underage drinking. They might see inappropriate sexual content. They might see a completely immature and irresponsible person. If they see any of that, they'll be inclined to cross off the recruit. And you know what? That's fine. Don't be stupid or you'll face the consequences. This is true for every young person, including my own kids.

I'm not unsympathetic here. I know it's a lot harder being young today than it was for my generation. There was no permanent record of the views we shared. No one can hold the remarks we made against us because right after we said those things they immediately became part of the past. Nowadays it's a different story. The past stays with you forever. So you better be responsible.

But still, there's a wide gap between acting like an idiot and offering a critical view of amateurism. The NCAA likes to conflate the two when they shouldn't.

One approach to more effectively—and more fairly—regulating the use of social media by college athletes would be for the NCAA and colleges to draft social media policies in consultation with the athletes themselves. They are clearly stakeholders. They also, frankly, have a much better sense of the culture of social media than we older folks do. Bring everyone together and put together sensible rules.

8. Schedule games and practices in reasonable ways given college athletes' academic requirements.

Years ago, college conferences were designed with geography as a primary consideration. This made sense, as travel impacts college athletes' ability to attend class and study. Tradition and cultural rivalries also played roles in conference configurations.

My friends from the former Big East know that all too well. But even then, geography had always been a crucial consideration.

More recently, though, conferences and their membership have placed proximity on the back burner. They have instead made television interests their number-one priority. The fact is that conferences are increasingly designed to advance broadcasting contracts, irrespective of distance between schools in a conference.

This practice has meant very, very long trips for college athletes, who, we should remember, are supposed to be college students.

Take the Big Ten Conference, which spans from Nebraska to New Jersey. That's right. Colleges located in states stretching from Nebraska to New Jersey are in the same grouping. This means that in the middle of the semester, the Nebraska Cornhuskers have to travel 1,300 miles to play the Rutgers Scarlet Knights. Then they have to travel another 1,300 miles to return home so they can attend their classes and take exams.

Even more geographically jarring is Conference USA, which extends from Texas to West Virginia. Two of its members, the University of Texas at El Paso Miners and the Florida International University Panthers, need to fly nearly 1,900 miles so they can play each other.

Does that make any sense?

This kind of disruptive and lengthy travel makes it extra hard for college athletes to study and to meet the academic requirements of being full-time students.

Look, it's hard enough to spend forty to fifty hours per week on games, practices, and team meetings. Then athletes are expected to compete against classmates who, in most cases, don't work and are usually forbidden from working more than twenty hours a week. On top of that, five-hour flights across the country are added to the equation. It is really adding insult to injury.

So where is the NCAA in this discussion? The NCAA has conveniently left conference membership up to member institutions. As a result, NCAA realignment has run rampant as better financial deals surface. Schools are obsessed with access to lucrative TV markets and fertile recruiting territories. They are willing to spend money on travel if it means expanding their fan base to other parts of the country and bringing in more money.

Lost in this quest for the almighty dollar are the college athletes. They are increasingly placed on cross-country flights and seated on multihour bus rides, sometimes multiple times per week.

It isn't right.

If the NCAA wants to advance an honest, defensible version of amateurism, it should regulate conference realignment. And it should do so with students' interests in mind and with the advice of those students, too.

The NCAA isn't afraid of aggressively pursuing a goal while claiming it's for the good of the athlete.

So how about it takes that attitude with a topic that actually relates to the good of the athlete?

9. End fake NCAA rules and policies, like the "twenty-hour per week" rule.

The NCAA loves rules. That's okay, so long as the rules are fair and honest. Therein lies a big problem. The NCAA has enacted a number of rules that we might say rely on alternative facts.

Take the NCAA rule that student-athletes can engage in only four hours per day and twenty hours per week of so-called "countable athletically related activities" during the season. These activities include playing games, participating in practices, attending meetings that are initiated by coaches, and complying with required weight training.

The twenty-hour rule, however, doesn't include travel or "voluntary" activities. These are sizable exceptions. Earlier I detailed the extent and frequency of cross-country travel by college athletes. As to "voluntary" activities, let me tell you something: what's technically "voluntary" may not seem it to a teenage athlete who's trying to impress his or her coach and who is often afraid of that coach.

The reality is that college athletes spend closer to fifty hours per week on sports during the season. This is no secret. Just ask any college athlete at a Division I school and he or she will tell you.

So why is there a discrepancy between an NCAA rule and a college sports reality? Part of it reflects how hours are counted. Compliance officers track violations of the twenty-hour rule and are supposed to report violations to the NCAA. These officers use software to collect the relevant data. Sounds organized, right? Well, this is actually an imprecise approach for a number of reasons. A big one is that countable hours are submitted by coaches and approved by players.

Could you imagine a college player telling the coach that the hours are listed incorrectly? Yeah, right. Good luck with that. If there's one person you *don't* correct as a college athlete, it's your coach.

Plus, compliance officers often have to track down coaches and students to find out the hours. Sometimes those hours aren't submitted for days or even weeks later, at which point they are complete guesstimates.

This system creates a farce. Just be honest with the hours. Recognize the enormous sacrifice that college athletes undertake to represent their schools in athletic events while simultaneously balancing a full-time course load, not to mention trying to enjoy at least a little of the college experience enjoyed by their classmates.

I realize this is a sensitive topic for the NCAA. In their

petition to the National Labor Relations Board, Northwestern University football players argued that because their time in sports amounted to a full-time job, they ought to be recognized as Northwestern employees. The NCAA doesn't want to see that argument used in other legal pursuits.

But let's be real. If the NCAA is concerned that changing the twenty-hour-per-week rule would make it easier for players to claim that they are employees, then the NCAA has the wrong priorities.

The NCAA shouldn't be worried about the legal ramifications of changing a fake rule into a real one. It should be worried about the students the NCAA is supposed to protect.

10. Let college athletes major in sports.

Last summer UCLA quarterback Josh Rosen brought on some hate while simultaneously making many UCLA alums like myself proud. How did that happen? My man Josh spoke the truth about amateurism!

"Look," Rosen said at the time. "Football and school don't go together. They just don't. Trying to do both is like trying to do two full-time jobs. There are guys who have no business being in school, but they're here because this is the path to the NFL. There's no other way."

Rosen's views get at the fundamental tension of being a college athlete. There's simply too much to do and not enough time. Taking a full course load while spending fifty hours a week on sports creates a nearly impossible situation. It's one that makes athletes feel they have no chance to compete academically.

I've seen the effects of this firsthand. College athletes start to doubt their intellectual abilities and they start to believe they will fail. This creates a self-fulfilling prophecy: I believe many athletes fail in college largely because they think they will fail. It is well known in education that low expectations lead to low results. Downward spirals can be vicious.

I realize that there are different ways we could go about trying to fix this problem. But try this one out: allow college athletes to major in sports.

You might say that sounds crazy. I can hear you: *O'Bannon, what are you thinking, my man?*

Just hold on a second.

Do you feel the same way about students who major in drama? Or how about art majors? Or dance majors? Or some other skill-based major that is completely different from those students studying traditional liberal arts and science?

The thing is, athletics are just like dance and art in that they involve natural abilities that can be enhanced through hard work, practice, and coaching. If all goes well, these abilities can even be turned into a career.

But majoring in sports wouldn't only involve developing athletic talent. It would also entail developing the brain. To that end, sports majors would learn about the history and ethics of sports and competition. They would also study related—and important—issues of justice and fairness.

I'd also want to see those majoring in sports gain real training in skills that would help them as professionals. To that end, finance, accounting, and marketing classes would be essential. I know I wish I had taken those in college. Managing money and understanding how contracts are negotiated are critical skills in any sports career. Yet many college athletes get no training in them whatsoever. Communication courses would also be beneficial in trying to manage a public persona. These days an athlete can destroy his or her career with the wrong tweet or post. Once the wrong message is out, it often can't be walked back. Also, I see that some sports management programs offer sports coaching courses—those would be another element of a major in sports. I discuss them in more detail in my recommendation number 11, where I advocate for degrees in coaching. Coaching courses would also highlight a potential alternative career path.

There are many possibilities for a major focused on sports. Students could learn a great deal and also become better prepared to enter the sports industry, be it as a player, coach, or team official.

I realize the NCAA would probably object to this idea. The argument would be, in so many words, that a student-athlete majoring in sports would be wasting their education if they never became a pro.

This is really a weak argument on at least three levels.

First, that type of standard isn't applied to music and drama majors. Did all of John Mayer's classmates at the Berklee College of Music in Boston become professional musicians? How about Angela Bassett's classmates at the Yale School of Drama—did each one find his or her way to Hollywood or Broadway? We know the answer to those questions. And it isn't used to delegitimize those degree programs.

Second, there are all sorts of careers in sports that extend beyond playing. Coaching is an obvious one, and so too are sports marketing and promotion positions. And, although I've raised concerns about NCAA compliance, compliance officers are engaged in careers that could be enhanced by having majored in sports. The bottom line is that you don't have to play sports to enjoy a great career in sports.

And, third, think of the psychological benefits of offering a major in which college athletes would be well positioned to thrive. They would know the degree program would be relevant to them and that it would offer them training in topics of genuine interest. When you are passionate about a topic, you are much more likely to excel at understanding it. Earlier, I talked about the self-fulfilling prophecy of failure. Well, how about one for success? How about an upward spiral instead of a downward one? College athletes would do well as sports majors at least in part because they would believe they would do well. That counts for something. Let's not ignore it.

So let's make degree programs relevant to college athletes and help them succeed both in school and their careers that follow.

11. Develop educational programs to help former college athletes break into coaching and become better able to stop bullying, hazing, and domestic violence.

Earlier I discussed my interest in becoming a college basketball coach and some of the challenges I've faced in pursuing that career. Being the guy who sued the NCAA doesn't exactly make for great small talk in interviews! I still hope that one day a school gives me an opportunity. I know I'd have a lot to share. But in the meantime, I'm going to advocate for others who want to break into coaching. To that end, I'd like to see schools add degree programs in coaching.

I realize that several existing degree programs, like those in sports science and physical education majors, already offer important insights for prospective coaches. And I know various organizations, including USA Hockey and AAU basketball, train and certify coaches. But what I'm talking about is a standalone major in coaching and a postgraduate program as well.

These programs would obviously offer courses on coaching techniques. Designing plays is truly an art. The same goes for communicating with players. Natural ability no doubt matters, but that is true in any academic field, be it political science, history, or math. Education in any field makes one better at it.

A degree program, though, should also offer critical education on the many facets of coaching that go well beyond X's and O's and motivating players.

Look, a good coach is one who wins games. A great one is one who does that but is also able to detect and take action against wrongful conduct.

Take bullying and hazing. Both unfortunately occur in college athletic programs. Bullying sometimes refers to what we understood the word to mean back when I was young: physically intimidating another person in order to demean them and take advantage of them. But as social media has become a major part of young adults' lives, the means of bullying have only multiplied. These days bullying can occur when one person sends hateful texts to another person. It also takes place when one person ridicules someone else on Facebook or Twitter, for the entire world to see. It can be brutal and shaming.

Prospective coaches should be formally trained to deal with bullying. Using common sense doesn't always lead to the right answer. We should all listen to what the experts say and heed their advice.

The same is true for bullying's even more grotesque cousin, hazing.

I thankfully never experienced hazing in high school or college, and I never partook in it either. I guess the closest I came to being hazed was when I was a rookie on the Nets in 1995. Rick Mahorn had me bring in donuts a couple of times and told me to mop up Gatorade on the floor. Rick also had me buy cigars for him. I never thought of those things as hazing, especially since Rick was the one person on the Nets who took me under his wing and genuinely cared for me. And, frankly, having to go to Dunkin' Donuts before practice on a few occasions was the least of my worries while I was on the Nets!

But others in sports aren't so lucky. I remember the hazing scandal at Northwestern University involving the women's soccer team. It was widely covered, including by ABC News and the *New York Times*. It took place about a dozen years ago. Photographs of the women being hazed went online. They were photos of the athletes blindfolded, paraded around mostly naked, and with their hands tied behind their backs. Many of the young women's bodies had been covered in marker. They appeared to be forced to drink and perform lap dances, too.

It was outrageous and disgusting, not to mention very dangerous. I saw it through the eyes of both a former athlete and a dad whose daughter would play college sports. It takes an awful lot to make me angry, but that sure did.

The Northwestern soccer coach, Jenny Haigh, resigned, but it's a problem that isn't entirely repaired by a coach's exit. Hazing is a cultural issue on campuses that is passed down through generations. It's as if the tribal instinct of humans honed thousands of years ago resurfaces in certain situations.

And what happens when photos like those from Northwestern *aren't* posted online? Does it take a college athlete dying or being maimed by some hazing ritual for it to become known? And will every hazed player feel the courage to tell others, or will they feel too afraid?

We know the answer to these questions, and they are troubling.

As I mentioned earlier, the coach is only part of the hazing puzzle. But a coach who is trained in how to detect signs of hazing is a better coach. An even better coach is one who has learned about the best means of sensing signs or hints of hazing activities and then knows what to do about them. *That* coach is the one who reduces the risk of hazing from ever happening. A coaching degree program would include training along those lines.

The same goes for perhaps the most worrisome issue for college coaches today: stopping players from sexually assaulting classmates and holding players who perpetrate those crimes accountable.

I don't know if times have changed or if I was in a fortunate place or if I simply didn't see what was happening around me, but I didn't experience any incidents at UCLA where a teammate or another Bruins athlete was accused of sexual assault.

And it wasn't for a lack of sample size.

Outside of my time at home while recuperating from knee surgery, I lived on campus my first two years. And, yes, I went to many parties, including fraternity parties, during that stretch.

It goes without saying, but when you're at a party or some other get-together, your window into what's taking place around you is limited to what you see, hear, and otherwise sense. A lot might be occurring outside of that limited perspective. So what we perceive is by no means a full picture.

That said, other than a few fistfights between guys who were living in dorms and suites, I really didn't see anything resembling violence. Maybe I was fortunate or maybe I wasn't, as we say these days, "woke" to my surroundings. I'm not sure. Either way, my college experience didn't include knowing athletes who were accused of legal wrongdoing.

Unfortunately, the same isn't true for quite a few college athletes these days. It seems that every week or two there's a new report of college athletes being accused of committing sexual assault. The report also shows that these athletes' universities responded passively or, worse yet, enabled the crimes to happen.

Baylor University. University of Tennessee. Florida State University. University of Richmond. The list goes on and on.

And the allegations—in some cases criminal convictions—are truly horrible. They almost all involve college athletes getting young women drunk or drugging them and then raping them, sometimes in a group "gang rape" style.

And in each instance the university somehow failed in its duty to protect.

Coaches fail to report the allegations to their superiors. Athletic staff members refuse to share important details with student conduct officers. Athletes agree to lie about and defame the victim as a way of intimidating her so she might remain silent.

When you put these things together, you get athletes who feel that they can get away with sexual assault.

And that is simply inexcusable.

For its part, the NCAA hasn't sanctioned schools over their players committing sexual assault. Sure, the NCAA sanctions schools for recruits receiving free meals. And, yes, schools that fail to stop their unpaid players from accepting "gifts" are serious rule violators in the eyes of the NCAA. But schools whose players sexually assault young women and who help those players cover up their crimes? That apparently doesn't show a "lack of institutional control," to borrow NCAA language. It's all head-scratching, if you ask me.

These are problems that, to fix, would require many levers being pulled. There's no simple solution here.

But coaches can nonetheless play a major role. Many of them, like me, have children who went away to college. Coaches should use all the parenting skills in their bodies and souls to educate these young men and women on what it takes to become adults.

For some players, maybe that means sitting them down, one on one, and teaching each about why it's so important to stay clear of trouble. They need to hear how their decisions today will impact them for decades to come. For other players, the best approach might mean praying with them on the virtuous life that God wants all of us to lead.

The key is that the coach talks to his or players, and not just about sports, either. Morality and ethical judgment are just as, if not more, important topics for a coach to teach.

So how we do train better coaches so they make their players into better people? A degree program in coaching would go a long way. And if that program takes the form of a graduate degree, the NCAA would do the right thing by helping former athletes pay for it.

12. Give college athletes a say on who becomes— and remains—NCAA president.

My final proposal is simple and impactful: empower college athletes to have actual say on NCAA leadership.

Currently, the NCAA's Board of Governors hires the NCAA president and other NCAA executives and decides whether to keep them in their jobs. This means the NCAA's president must be on good terms with the Board of Governors; if not, the president can be fired.

So who is on this Board of Governors? The Board has sixteen voting members. All of them are college presidents or university chancellors. The Board also has four nonvoting members. They include the NCAA president, two athletic directors, and a dean of students.

Notice who's *not* on the Board of Governors: student-athletes and former student-athletes.

In an ideal world, they would be. It would make sense, too.

After all, athletes are unquestionably major stakeholders in NCAA policies and strategies. And the board is, in its own words, the "highest governance body in the NCAA" and "charged with ensuring that each division operates consistently with the basic purposes, fundamental policies and general principles of the Association." Shouldn't athletes have a voice on those "basic purposes, fundamental policies and general principles"?

If the NCAA won't go for adding athletes to the Board,

then at least let athletes—both current and former—vote on NCAA leadership.

During this decade, there has been no one more influential over college athletes than Mark Emmert. And yet under the NCAA's framework, he owes nothing to those athletes. He doesn't report to them. He doesn't talk with them. He doesn't have to worry about them in any shape or form. He only needs to please a board that, as currently configured, is essentially an echo chamber for university leaders.

Depriving athletes of any role is why the NCAA finds itself in the mess it's in. NCAA policies are shaped by people whose interests are often not aligned with the athletes'. In many cases, those interests are in conflict.

Think about the views of a random college president on whether athletes should be able to license their names, images, and likenesses. I can't speak for a college president, but I suspect those views would not place the point of emphasis on athletes' wellbeing and fairness to those athletes. It would instead focus on the financial impact on a school.

Now you might argue, *Wait a second, Ed. In professional sports, players don't have a say in who becomes commissioner or in whether that person remains commissioner. So why are you saying college athletes should be able to have that say?*

You would be correct about pro athletes. But what you'd be missing is that pro athletes have unions, and they're called players' associations, or PAs. These PAs collectively bargain workplace rules with leagues. They also fight to ensure that athletes' legal rights are protected.

PAs have a long history in pro sports. They have bargained for free agency because of the courage of former Major League Baseball player Curt Flood. In 1969 Flood sued the MLB after mailing a letter to MLB commissioner Bowie Kuhn in which the thirty-one-year-old center fielder wrote, "After twelve years in the Major Leagues, I do not feel I am a piece of property to be bought and sold irrespective of my wishes." Talk about bravery. Flood didn't win his case, but he began a cause that later proved victorious and inspired many other athletes, including me.

And a year later, Oscar Robertson filed his antitrust, class-action suit through the National Basketball Players Association, which, as I've mentioned earlier, was the first crack in the armor of the reserve clause that had long bound professional athletes to one team.

PAs have also bargained for economic terms that guarantee that pro athletes' names, images, and likenesses are licensed in ways that give athletes a voice and fair compensation. And although pro athletes don't pick the commissioner, they do pick their PA's counterpart—the executive director—as well as various other union leaders. In other words, pro athletes have an actual say regarding their rights because those athletes can form unions.

But college athletes can't. At least for now, college athletes aren't considered employees under federal law.

Perhaps that will change at some point.

But in the meantime, the NCAA would be wise to open up their closed tent. Let the athletes in. Stop viewing them as the enemy or the servants. Treat them as partners.

And trust me, *everyone*, including the NCAA, would be much better off.

EPILOGUE

"COME ON, EDWARD, YOU'VE GOT THIS!"

I smiled when I heard Rosa yell those words as we sat in the stands of Klein Family Field in Stockton, California. This took place on one of our recent visits there to see our youngest son, Edward III, pitch for the University of Pacific Tigers.

Strike.

Edward was on the mound. His first pitch was a sharp slider that hit the corner of the strike zone.

And it all felt so right. We were two parents watching our child on the ball field. That's all we were. Eating popcorn while sipping water, and wearing our Tigers ball caps.

I'm sure Edward would say he didn't notice us, but he knew we were sitting there. He knew his mom, who's not exactly a sports fan, was totally into it.

At the opening of the John Wooden Library and UCLA Hall of Fame. My kids: Aaron, Jazmin, and Ed III.

There were only a few hundred people sitting in the ballpark that day. I bet not one of them was thinking very much about money in college sports. And if the law was on anyone's mind, it had nothing to do with the game.

This was life in an American ballpark and college sports in its truest form.

All we saw was our big "little" man making his parents proud. Edward now stands six foot seven and is muscular, too. But Rosa and I remember when he was just a little guy who loved to play catch with his dad in our back yard.

Edward took after me in that regard. If you asked anyone from my neighborhood growing up which was my best sport, they would tell you baseball. Hands down. Back in the day I was a pitcher—a tall, lanky, left-handed pitcher. I threw gas. I could really dial it up. And I loved the sport, too. Still do—everything about baseball. From the crack of the bat, to the sound of the cleats, to the smell of the grass while playing day games, to the lights that bring life to night games. The deliberate pace of the game captures you, and the smell of the leather on your mitt keeps you. And there's nothing like the feel of a baseball and gripping it. It's almost magical that how you grip a baseball completely changes its trajectory once it leaves your hand.

As a kid I dreamed sometimes of playing for the Lakers, but that wasn't the dream I had most often. No, it was to pitch for the Los Angeles Dodgers. I wanted to grow up and be their ace.

But my baseball dreams started to fade as I shot up in height. By the time I was fifteen I had grown to six foot eight. Everybody thought I would focus on basketball. And so I did. It's kind of funny. The way people look at you as an athlete can alter which sport you focus on and your life as a result.

Well, I wasn't going to let that happen with Edward. We knew he would be tall. We also knew that people would assume he'd follow in the footsteps of his dad and sister and pursue hoops. But Rosa and I looked at it differently. Edward's heart was in baseball. He had that same passion like I did. We weren't going to let it go away.

Strike two.

Boom. Edward blows that fastball right by the batter. Does it get any better? If there is such a thing as a cloud nine, I was on it. That's *my* son out there—I'm *his* dad.

So, yes, I'm Ed O'Bannon. I'm the guy who saw himself in a college basketball video game and then brought a lawsuit over it. I'm the guy who knew he'd never get a dollar from the case but might change rules to help out others. I'm the guy who NCAA employees testified against in court and who NCAA lawyers tried to cut down on the witness stand.

Yeah, I'm that guy.

But don't think for a second that I don't love college sports. Just the opposite. There's no better level of athletics than at the college level. It's where I became a man years ago. It's where I'm a father now.

I just want fairness. That's all. The NCAA should treat people—student-athletes, college athletes, or whatever label you prefer to describe these extraordinarily gifted young men and women—as they should be treated.

And you know what? If that happens, then everyone at a college game will be focused on what they see in front of them, and on what they hear, and on what they feel.

Strike three, you're out!

"Yeah, Little Ed, that's my boy!"

ACKNOWLEDGMENTS

THANKS TO MY WONDERFUL WIFE AND BEST FRIEND, ROSA, WHO is everything in the world to me and whose contributions to this book have been invaluable and inspiring; to our three amazing children—Aaron, Jazmin, and Edward—each of whom has made Rosa and me so proud; to my parents, Madelyn and Edward, Sr., for always believing in me and raising me right; to my brother, Charles, for always having my back; to the coaches who spent countless hours with me on my game and who always encouraged me to succeed; and to the late and great Rich Abajian for giving this ex-jock a chance and taking me under his wings—Rich, I'll see you again in Heaven.

—Ed O'Bannon

THANKS TO KARA, MY AMAZING WIFE AND POSSIBLY THE BEST AMateur proofreader on Earth; to my parents, Jill and Bill, for encouraging me to aim high and never be deterred by the possibility of falling short; to my siblings—Maria, Melissa and Bill—for always making time for their kid brother; to my research assistant, Zach Leach, for his perceptiveness and dedication; and to Winston, an extraordinary Welsh Corgi who knows how to cheer anyone up.

—Michael McCann

INDEX

ABOUT THE AUTHORS

ED O'BANNON led the UCLA men's basketball team to the 1995 NCAA Basketball Championship. He received the NCAA Tournament's Most Outstanding Player Award and won numerous other awards, including the John Wooden Award and the Oscar Robertson Trophy, both of which recognize the best college basketball player in the country.

O'Bannon was the ninth player selected in the 1995 NBA draft and enjoyed a ten-year professional basketball career. After retiring from the game, O'Bannon entered the car dealership industry. In 2009, he filed a federal lawsuit against the NCAA and Electronic Arts. In a landmark decision, which was upheld by the US Court of Appeals, O'Bannon defeated the NCAA. He received no compensation from the case. O'Bannon, who is from Los Angeles, now resides in Henderson, Nevada, with his wife, Rosa. They have three children.

MICHAEL McCANN is *Sports Illustrated*'s legal analyst and has authored more than six hundred articles for *SI*. He is also the Associate Dean for Academic Affairs, a professor of law, with tenure, and Director of the Sports and Entertainment Law Institute at the University of New Hampshire School of Law. He is the editor of the *Oxford Handbook of American Sports Law* and has authored articles in the *Yale Law Journal, Boston College Law Review*, and *Harvard Journal of Sports and Entertainment Law*, among other top law reviews. He holds degrees from Harvard Law School, the University of Virginia School of Law, and Georgetown University. McCann resides in his hometown of Andover, Massachusetts, with his wife, Kara.